essentialism

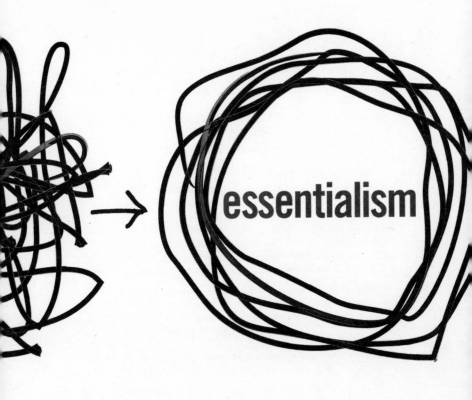

essentialism

The Disciplined Pursuit of Less

GREG McKEOWN

10

First published in the United States by Crown Business

An imprint of Crown Publishing Group, a division of Random House LLC

First published in the United Kingdom in 2014 by Virgin Books, an imprint of Ebury Publishing

A Random House Group Company

Copyright © 2014 by Greg McKeown

Addresses for companies within The Random House Group Limited can be found at www.randomhouse.co.uk/offices.htm

The Random House Group Limited Reg. No. 954009

A CIP catalogue record for this book is available from the British Library

Penguin Random House is committed to a sustainable future for our business, our readers and our planet. This book is made from Forest Stewardship Council® certified paper.

Printed and bound in Great Britain by Clays Ltd, St Ives plc

ISBN: 9780753555163

To buy books by your favourite authors and register for offers, visit www. randomhouse.co.uk

CONTENTS

CHAPTER 1

The Essentialist

THE WISDOM OF LIFE CONSISTS IN THE
ELIMINATION OF NON-ESSENTIALS.

—*Lin Yutang*

Sam Elliot* is a capable executive in Silicon Valley, California, who found himself stretched too thin after his company was acquired by a larger, bureaucratic business.

He was in earnest about being a good citizen in his new role so he said *yes* to many requests without really thinking about it. But as a result he would spend the whole day rushing from one meeting and conference call to another trying to please everyone and get it all done. His stress went up as the quality of his work went down. It was like he was majoring in minor activities and as a result, his work became unsatisfying for him *and* frustrating for the people he was trying so hard to please.

* Name has been changed.

In the midst of his frustration the company came to him and offered him an early retirement package. But he was in his early 50s and had no interest in completely retiring. He thought briefly about starting a consulting company doing what he was already doing. He even thought of selling his services back to his employer as a consultant. But none of these options seemed that appealing. So he went to speak with a mentor who gave him surprising advice: "Stay, but do what you would as a consultant and nothing else. And don't tell anyone." In other words, his mentor was advising him to do only those things that *he* deemed essential – and ignore everything else that was asked of him.

The executive followed the advice! He made a daily commitment towards cutting out the red tape. He began saying no.

He was tentative at first. He would evaluate requests based on the timid criteria, "Can I actually fulfil this request, given the time and resources I have?" If the answer was *no* then he would refuse the request. He was pleasantly surprised to find that while people would at first look a little disappointed, they seemed to respect his honesty.

Encouraged by his small wins he pushed back a bit more. Now when a request would come in he would pause and evaluate the request against a tougher criteria: "Is this the very *most* important thing I should be doing with my time and resources right now?"

If he couldn't answer a definitive *yes,* then he would refuse the request. And once again to his delight, while his colleagues might initially seem disappointed, they soon began to respect him *more* for his refusal, not less.

Emboldened, he began to apply this selective criteria to everything, not just direct requests. In his past life he would always volunteer for presentations or assignments that came up last minute;

now he found a way not to sign up for them. He used to be one of the first to jump in on an e-mail trail, but now he just stepped back and let others jump in. He stopped attending conference calls that he only had a couple of minutes of interest in. He stopped sitting in on the weekly update call because he didn't need the information. He stopped attending meetings on his calendar if he didn't have a direct contribution to make. He explained to me, "Just because I was invited didn't seem a good enough reason to attend."

It felt self-indulgent at first. But by being selective he bought himself space, and in that space he found creative freedom. He could concentrate his efforts on one project at a time. He could plan thoroughly. He could anticipate roadblocks and start to re-move obstacles. Instead of spinning his wheels trying to get eve-rything done, he could get the right things done. His newfound commitment to doing only the things that were truly important – and eliminating everything else – restored the quality of his work. Instead of making just a millimetre of progress in a million di-rections he began to generate tremendous momentum towards ac-complishing the things that were truly vital.

He continued this for several months. He immediately found that he not only got more of his day back at work, in the evenings he got even more time back at home. He said, "I got back my family life! I can go home at a decent time." Now instead of being a slave to his phone he shuts it down. He goes to the gym. He goes out to eat with his wife.

To his great surprise, there were no negative repercussions to his experiment. His manager didn't chastise him. His colleagues didn't resent him. Quite the opposite; because he was left only with projects that were meaningful to him *and* actually valuable to the company, they began to respect and value his work more than ever.

His work became fulfilling again. His performance ratings went up. He ended up with one of the largest bonuses of his career!

In this example is the basic value proposition of Essentialism: only once you give yourself permission to stop trying to do it all, to stop saying yes to everyone, can you make your highest contribution towards the things that really matter.

What about you? How many times have you reacted to a request by saying yes without really thinking about it? How many times have you resented committing to do something and wondered, "Why did I sign up for this?" How often do you say yes simply to please? Or to avoid trouble? Or because "yes" had just become your default response?

Now let me ask you this: Have you ever found yourself stretched too thin? Have you ever felt both overworked *and* underutilised? Have you ever found yourself majoring in minor activities? Do you ever feel busy but not productive? Like you're always in motion, but never getting anywhere?

If you answered yes to any of these, the way out is the way of the Essentialist.

The Way of the Essentialist

Dieter Rams was the lead designer at Braun for many years. He is driven by the idea that almost everything is noise. He believes very few things are essential. His job is to filter through that noise until he gets to the essence. For example, as a young twenty-four-year-old at the company he was asked to collaborate on a record player. The norm at the time was to cover the turntable in a solid wooden lid or even to incorporate the player into a piece of living room furniture. Instead, he and his team removed the clutter and designed a player with a clear plastic cover on the top and nothing more. It was the first time such a design had been used, and it was so revolutionary people worried it might bankrupt the company because nobody would buy it. It took courage, as it always does, to eliminate the non-essential. By the sixties this aesthetic started to gain traction. In time it became the design every other record player followed.

Dieter's design criteria can be summarised by a characteristically succinct principle, captured in just three German words: *Weniger aber besser.* The English translation is: *Less but better.* A more fitting definition of Essentialism would be hard to come by.

The way of the Essentialist is the relentless pursuit of less but better. It doesn't mean occasionally giving a nod to the principle. It means pursuing it in a *disciplined* way.

The way of the Essentialist isn't about setting New Year's resolutions to say "no" more, or about pruning your in-box, or about mastering some new strategy in time management. It is about pausing constantly to ask, "Am I investing in the right activities?" There are far more activities and opportunities in the world than we have time and resources to invest in. And although many of them may be good, or even very good, the fact is that most are trivial and few are vital. The way of the Essentialist involves learning to tell the difference – learning to filter through all those options and selecting only those that are truly essential.

Essentialism is not about how to get more things done; it's about how to get the *right* things done. It doesn't mean just doing less for the sake of less either. It is about making the wisest possible investment of your time and energy in order to operate at your highest point of contribution by doing only what is essential.

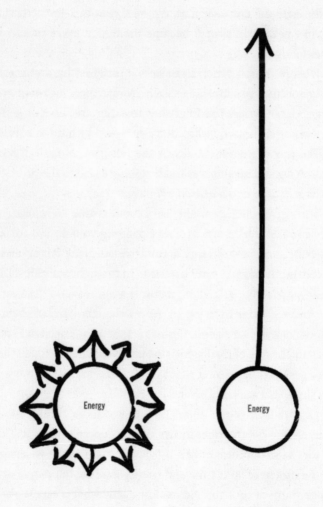

The difference between the way of the Essentialist and the way of the non-Essentialist can be seen in the figure opposite. In both images the same amount of effort is exerted. In the image on the left, the energy is divided into many different activities. The result is that we have the unfulfilling experience of making a millimetre of progress in a million directions. In the image on the right, the energy is given to fewer activities. The result is that by investing in fewer things we have the satisfying experience of making significant progress in the things that matter most. The way of the Essentialist rejects the idea that we can fit it all in. Instead it requires us to grapple with real trade-offs and make tough decisions. In many cases we can learn to make one-time decisions that make a thousand future decisions so we don't exhaust ourselves asking the same questions again and again.

The way of the Essentialist means living by design, not by default. Instead of making choices reactively, the Essentialist deliberately distinguishes the vital few from the trivial many, eliminates the non-essentials, and then removes obstacles so the essential things have clear, smooth passage. In other words, Essentialism is a disciplined, systematic approach for determining where our highest point of contribution lies, then making execution of those things almost effortless.

The Model

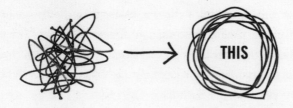

	Non-Essentialist	**Essentialist**
Thinks	**ALL THINGS TO ALL PEOPLE** "I have to." "It's all important." "How can I fit it all in?"	**LESS BUT BETTER** "I choose to." "Only a few things really matter." "What are the trade-offs?"
Does	**THE UNDISCIPLINED PURSUIT OF MORE** Reacts to what's most pressing Says "yes" to people without really thinking Tries to force execution at the last moment	**THE DISCIPLINED PURSUIT OF LESS** Pauses to discern what really matters Says "no" to everything except the essential Removes obstacles to make execution easy
Gets	**LIVES A LIFE THAT DOES NOT SATISFY** Takes on too much, and work suffers Feels out of control Is unsure of whether the right things got done Feels overwhelmed and exhausted	**LIVES A LIFE THAT REALLY MATTERS** Chooses carefully in order to do great work Feels in control Gets the right things done Experiences joy in the journey

The way of the Essentialist is the path to being in control of our own choices. It is a path to new levels of success and meaning. It is the path on which we enjoy the journey, not just the destination. Despite all these benefits, however, there are too many forces conspiring to keep us from applying the disciplined pursuit of less but better, which may be why so many end up on the misdirected path of the non-Essentialist.

The Way of the Non-Essentialist

On a bright, winter day in California I visited my wife, Anna, in hospital. Even in hospital Anna was radiant. But I also knew she was exhausted. It was the day after our precious daughter was born, healthy and happy at 7 pounds, 3 ounces.[1]

Yet what should have been one of the happiest, most serene days of my life was actually filled with tension. Even as my beautiful new baby lay in my wife's tired arms, I was on the phone and on e-mail with work, and I was feeling pressure to go to a client meeting. My colleague had written, "Friday between 1–2 would be a bad time to have a baby because I need you to be at this meeting with X." It was now Friday and though I was pretty certain (or at least I hoped) the e-mail had been written in jest, I still felt pressure to attend.

Instinctively, I knew what to do. It was clearly a time to be there for my wife and newborn child. So when asked whether I planned to attend the meeting, I said with all the conviction I could muster . . .

"Yes."

To my shame, while my wife lay in hospital with our hours-old baby, I went to the meeting. Afterwards, my colleague said, "The client will respect you for making the decision to be here." But the look on the clients' faces did not evince respect. Instead, they mirrored how I felt. *What was I doing there?* I had said "yes" simply to please, and in doing so I had hurt my family, my integrity, and even the client relationship.

As it turned out, exactly *nothing* came of the client meeting. But even if it had, surely I would have made a fool's bargain. In trying to keep everyone happy I had sacrificed what mattered most.

On reflection I discovered this important lesson:

If you don't prioritise your life, someone else will.

That experience gave me renewed interest – read, inexhaustible obsession – in understanding why otherwise intelligent people make the choices they make in their personal and professional lives. "Why is it," I wonder, "that we have so much more ability inside of us than we often choose to utilise?" And "How can we make the choices that allow us to tap into more of the potential inside ourselves, and in people everywhere?"

My mission to shed light on these questions had already led me to quit law school in England and travel, eventually, to California to do my graduate work at Stanford. It had led me to spend more than two years collaborating on a book, *Multipliers: How the Best Leaders Make Everyone Smarter.* And it went on to inspire me to start a strategy and leadership company in Silicon Valley, where I now work with some of the most capable people in some of the most interesting companies in the world, helping to set them on the path of the Essentialist.

In my work I have seen people all over the world who are consumed and overwhelmed by the pressures all around them. I have coached "successful" people in the quiet pain of trying desperately to do everything, perfectly, now. I have seen people trapped by controlling managers and unaware that they do not "have to" do all the thankless busywork they are asked to do. And I have worked tirelessly to understand *why* so many bright, smart, capable individuals remain snared in the death grip of the non-essential.

What I have found has surprised me.

I worked with one particularly driven executive who got into technology at a young age and loved it. He was quickly rewarded for his knowledge and passion with more and more opportunities. Eager to build on his success, he continued to read as much as he could and pursue all he could with gusto and enthusiasm. By the time I met him he was hyperactive, trying to learn it all and do it all. He seemed to find a new obsession every day, sometimes every hour. And in the process, he lost his ability to discern the vital few from the trivial many. *Everything* was important. As a result he was stretched thinner and thinner. He was making a millimetre of progress in a million directions. He was over-worked *and* underutilised. That's when I sketched out for him the image on the left in the figure on page 6.

He stared at it for the longest time in uncharacteristic silence. Then he said, with more than a hint of emotion, "That is the story of my life!" Then I sketched the image on the right. "What would happen if we could figure out the one thing you could do that would make the highest contribution?" I asked him. He responded sincerely: "That is *the* question."

As it turns out, many intelligent, ambitious people have perfectly legitimate reasons to have trouble answering this question. One reason is that in our society we are punished for good behaviour (saying no) and rewarded for bad behaviour (saying yes). The former is often awkward in the moment, and the latter is often celebrated in the moment. It leads to what I call "the paradox of success,"[2] which can be summed up in four predictable phases:

PHASE 1: When we really have clarity of purpose, it enables us to succeed at our endeavour.

PHASE 2: When we have success, we gain a reputation as a "go to" person. We become "good old [insert name]," who is always there when you need him, and we are presented with increased options and opportunities.

PHASE 3: When we have increased options and opportunities, which is actually code for demands upon our time and energies, it leads to diffused efforts. We get spread thinner and thinner.

PHASE 4: We become distracted from what would otherwise be our highest level of contribution. The effect of our success has been to undermine the very clarity that led to our success in the first place.

Curiously, and overstating the point in order to make it, *the pursuit of success can be a catalyst for failure*. Put another way, success can distract us from focusing on the essential things that produce success in the first place.

We can see this everywhere around us. In his book *How the Mighty Fall*, Jim Collins explores what went wrong in companies that were once darlings of Wall Street but later collapsed.[3] He finds that for many, falling into "the undisciplined pursuit of more" was a key reason for failure. This is true for companies and it is true for the people who work in them. But why?

Why Non-Essentialism Is Everywhere

Several trends have combined to create a perfect non-Essentialist storm. Consider the following.

TOO MANY CHOICES

We have all observed the exponential increase in choices over the last decade. Yet even in the midst of it, and perhaps because of it, we have lost sight of the most important ones.

As Peter Drucker said, "In a few hundred years, when the history of our time will be written from a long-term perspective, it is likely that the most important event historians will see is not technology, not the Internet, not e-commerce. It is an unprecedented change in the human condition. For the first time – literally – substantial and rapidly growing numbers of people have choices. For the first time, they will have to manage themselves. And society is totally unprepared for it."[4]

THE UNDISCIPLINED PURSUIT OF MORE

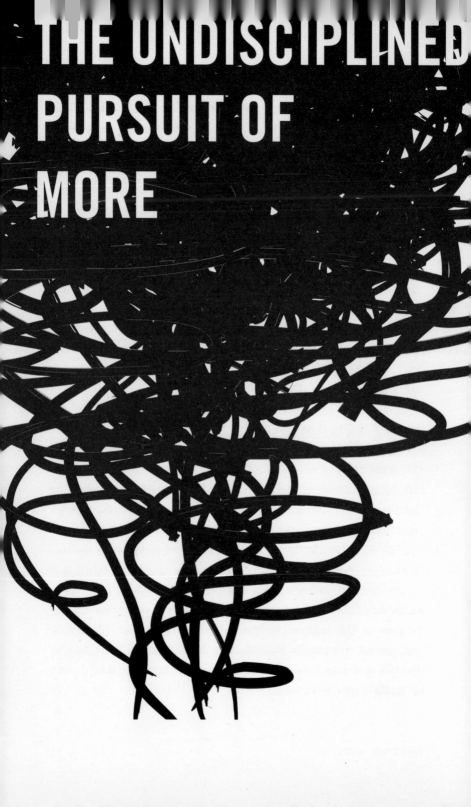

We are unprepared in part because, for the first time, the preponderance of choice has overwhelmed our ability to manage it. We have lost our ability to filter what is important and what isn't. Psychologists call this "decision fatigue": the more choices we are forced to make, the more the quality of our decisions deteriorates.[5]

TOO MUCH SOCIAL PRESSURE

It is not just the number of choices that has increased exponentially, it is also the strength and number of outside influences *on* our decisions that has increased. While much has been said and written about how hyperconnected we now are and how distracting this information overload can be, the larger issue is how our connectedness has increased the strength of social pressure. Today, technology has lowered the barrier for others to share their opinion about what we should be focusing on. It is not just information overload; it is opinion overload.

THE IDEA THAT "YOU CAN HAVE IT ALL"

The idea that we can have it all and do it all is not new. This myth has been peddled for so long, I believe virtually everyone alive today is infected with it. It is sold in advertising. It is championed in corporations. It is embedded in job descriptions that provide huge lists of required skills and experience as standard. It is embedded in university applications that require dozens of extracurricular activities.

What *is* new is how especially damaging this myth is today, in a time when choice and expectations have increased exponentially. It results in stressed people trying to cram yet *more* activities into their already overscheduled lives. It creates corporate environments that talk about work/life balance but still expect their employees to be on their smartphones 24/7/365. It leads to staff meetings where as many as ten "top priorities" are discussed with no sense of irony at all.

The word *priority* came into the English language in the 1400s. It was singular. It meant the very first or prior thing. It stayed singular for the next five hundred years. Only in the 1900s did we pluralise the term and start talking about *priorities*. Illogically, we reasoned that by changing the word we could bend reality. Somehow we would now be able to have multiple "first" things. People and companies routinely try to do just that. One leader told me of his experience in a company that talked of "Pri-1, Pri-2, Pri-3, Pri-4, and Pri-5." This gave the impression of many things being the priority but actually meant nothing was.

But when we try to do it all and have it all, we find ourselves making trade-offs at the margins that we would never take on as our intentional strategy. When we don't purposefully and deliberately choose where to focus our energies and time, other people – our bosses, our colleagues, our clients, and even our families – will choose for us, and before long we'll have lost sight of everything that is meaningful and important. We can either make our choices deliberately or allow other people's agendas to control our lives.

Once an Australian nurse named Bronnie Ware, who cared for people in the last twelve weeks of their lives, recorded their most often discussed regrets. At the top of the list: "I wish I'd had the courage to live a life true to myself, not the life others expected of me."[6]

This requires, not just haphazardly saying no, but purposefully, deliberately, and strategically eliminating the non-essentials, and not just getting rid of the obvious time wasters, but cutting out some really good opportunities as well.[7] Instead of reacting to the social pressures pulling you to go in a million directions, you will learn a way to reduce, simplify, and focus on what is absolutely essential by eliminating everything else.

You can think of this book doing for your life and career what a professional organiser can do for your wardrobe. Think about what happens to your wardrobe when you never organise it. Does it stay neat and tidy with just those few outfits you love to wear hanging on the rail? Of course not. When you make no conscious effort to keep it organised, the wardrobe becomes cluttered and stuffed with clothes you rarely wear. Every so often it gets so out of control you try and purge the wardrobe. But unless you have a disciplined system you'll either end up with as many clothes as you started with because you can't decide which to give away; end up with regrets because you accidentally gave away clothes you do wear and did want to keep; or end up with a pile of clothes you don't want to keep but never actually get rid of because you're not quite sure where to take them or what to do with them.

In the same way that our wardrobe get cluttered as clothes we never wear accumulate, so do our lives get cluttered as well-intended commitments and activities we've said yes to pile up. Most of these efforts didn't come with an expiry date. Unless we have a system for purging them, once adopted, they live on in perpetuity.

Here's how an Essentialist would approach that wardrobe.

1. EXPLORE AND EVALUATE

Instead of asking, "Is there a chance I will wear this someday in the future?" you ask more disciplined, tough questions: "Do I *love* this?" and "Do I look *great* in it?" and "Do I wear this *often*?" If the answer is no, then you know it is a candidate for elimination.

In your personal or professional life, the equivalent of asking yourself which clothes you love is asking yourself, "Will this activity or effort make the highest possible contribution towards my goal?" Part One of this book will help you figure out what those activities are.

2. ELIMINATE

Let's say you have your clothes divided into piles of "must keep" and "probably should get rid of." But are you really ready to stuff the "probably should get rid of" pile in a bag and send it off? After all, there is still a feeling of sunk-cost bias: studies have found that we tend to value things we already own more highly than they are worth and thus that we find them more difficult to get rid of. If you're not quite there, ask the killer question: "If I didn't already own this, how much would I spend to buy it?" This usually does the trick.

In other words, it's not enough to simply determine which activities and efforts don't make the highest possible contribution; you still have to actively eliminate those that do not. Part Two of this book will show you how to eliminate the non-essentials, and not only that, how do it in a way that garners you respect from colleagues, bosses, clients, and peers.

3. EXECUTE

If you want your wardrobe to stay tidy, you need a regular routine for organising it. You need one large bag for items you need to throw away and a very small pile for items you want to keep. You need to know the drop-off location and hours of your local charity shop. You need to have a scheduled time to go there.

In other words, once you've figured out which activities and efforts to keep – the ones that make your highest level of contribution – you need a system to make executing your intentions as effortless as possible. In this book you'll learn to create a process that makes getting the essential things done as effortless as possible.

Of course, our lives aren't static like the clothes in our wardrobe. Our clothes stay where they are once we leave them in the morning (unless we have teenagers!). But in the wardrobe of our lives, new clothes – new demands on our time – are coming at us constantly. Imagine if every time you opened the doors to your wardrobe you found that people had been shoving their clothes in there – if every day you cleaned it out in the morning and then by afternoon found it already stuffed to the brim. Unfortunately, most of our lives are much like this. How many times have you started your workday with a schedule and by 10 a.m. you were already completely off track or behind? Or how many times have you written a "to do" list in the morning but then found that by 5 p.m. the list was even *longer*? How many times have you looked forward to a quiet weekend at home with the family then found that by Saturday morning you were inundated with errands and play dates and unforeseen calamities? But here's the good news: there is a way out.

Essentialism is about creating a system for handling the wardrobe of our lives. This is not a process you undertake once a year, once a month, or even once a week, like organising your wardrobe. It is a *discipline* you apply each and every time you are faced with a decision about whether to say yes or whether to politely decline. It's a method for making the tough trade-off between lots of good things and a few really great things. It's about learning how to do less but better so you can achieve the highest possible return on every precious moment of your life.

This book will show you how to live a life true to yourself, not the life others expect from you. It will teach you a method for being more efficient, productive, and effective in both personal and professional realms. It will teach you a systematic way to discern what is important, eliminate what is not, and make doing the essential as effortless as possible. In short, it will teach you how to apply the disciplined pursuit of less to every area of your life. Here's how.

Road Map

There are four parts to the book. The first outlines the core mind-set of an Essentialist. The next three turn the mind-set into a systematic process for the disciplined pursuit of less, one you can use in any situation or endeavour you encounter. A description of each part of the book is below.

ESSENCE: WHAT IS THE CORE MIND-SET OF AN ESSENTIALIST?

This part of the book outlines the three realities without which Essentialist thinking would be neither relevant nor possible. One chapter is devoted to each of these in turn.

1. *Individual choice: We can choose how to spend our energy and time.* Without choice, there is no point in talking about trade-offs.

2. *The prevalence of noise: Almost everything is noise, and a very few things are exceptionally valuable.* This is the justification for taking time to figure out what is most important. Because some things *are* so much more important, the effort in finding those things is worth it.

3. *The reality of trade-offs: We can't have it all or do it all.* If we could, there would be no reason to evaluate or eliminate options. Once we accept the reality of trade-offs we stop asking, "How can I make it all work?" and start asking the more honest question "Which problem do I want to solve?"

Only when we understand these realities can we begin to think like an Essentialist. Indeed, once we fully accept and understand them, much of the method in the coming sections of the book becomes natural and instinctive. That method consists of the following three simple steps.

STEP 1. EXPLORE:
DISCERNING THE TRIVIAL MANY FROM THE VITAL FEW

One paradox of Essentialism is that Essentialists actually explore *more* options than their non-Essentialist counterparts. Whereas non-Essentialists commit to everything or virtually everything without actually exploring, Essentialists systematically explore and evaluate a broad set of options before committing to any. Because they will commit and "go big" on one or two ideas or activities, they deliberately explore more options at first to ensure that they pick the right one later.

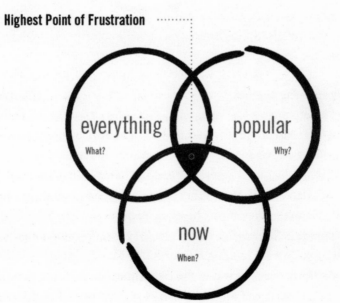

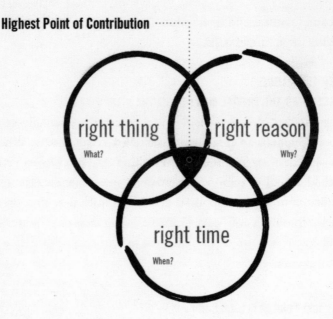

Highest Point of Contribution

right thing
What?

right reason
Why?

right time
When?

By applying tougher criteria we can tap into our brain's sophisticated search engine.[8] If we search for "a good opportunity," then we will find scores of pages for us to think about and work through. Instead, we can conduct an advanced search and ask three questions: "What do I feel deeply inspired by?" and "What am I particularly talented at?" and "What meets a significant need in the world?" Naturally there won't be as many pages to view, but this is the point of the exercise. We aren't looking for a plethora of good things to do. We are looking for our highest level of contribution: the right thing the right way at the right time.

Essentialists spend as much time as possible exploring, listening, debating, questioning, and thinking. But their exploration is not an end in itself. The purpose of the exploration is to discern the vital few from the trivial many.

STEP 2. ELIMINATE:
CUTTING OUT THE TRIVIAL MANY

Many of us say yes to things because we are eager to please and make a difference. Yet the key to making our highest contribution may well be saying no. As Peter Drucker said, "People are effective because they say 'no,' because they say, 'this isn't for me.'"[9]

To eliminate non-essentials means saying no *to* someone. Often. It means pushing against social expectations. To do it well takes courage *and* compassion. So eliminating the non-essentials isn't just about mental discipline. It's about the *emotional discipline* necessary to say no to social pressure. In this section of the book, we will address this challenging dynamic.

Given the reality of trade-offs, we can't choose to do everything. The real question is not how can we do it all, it is *who* will get to choose what we do and don't do. Remember, when we forfeit our right to choose, someone else will choose for us. So we can either deliberately choose what not to do or allow ourselves to be pulled in directions we don't want to go.

This section offers a method for eliminating the non-essentials, thus earning us the time necessary to achieve what is essential. Only then can we build a platform to make execution as effortless as possible: the subject of step 3.

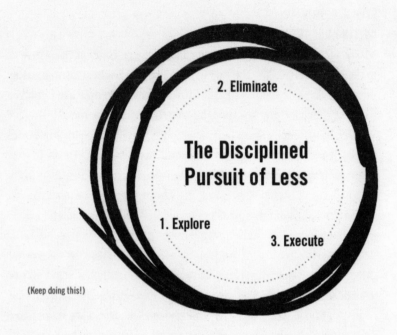

2. Eliminate

The Disciplined Pursuit of Less

1. Explore

3. Execute

(Keep doing this!)

STEP 3. EXECUTE:
REMOVING OBSTACLES AND MAKING EXECUTION EFFORTLESS

Whether our goal is to complete a project at work, reach the next step in our career, or plan a birthday party for our spouse, we tend to think of the process of execution as something hard and full of friction, something we need to force to "*make* happen." But the Essentialist approach is different. Instead of forcing execution, Essentialists invest the time they have saved into creating a system for removing obstacles and making execution as easy as possible.

These three elements – explore, eliminate, execute – are not separate events as much as a cyclical process. And when we apply them consistently we are able to reap greater and greater benefits.

An Idea Whose Time Has Come

As a quote attributed to Victor Hugo, the French dramatist and novelist, puts it, "Nothing is more powerful than an idea whose time has come." "Less but better" is a principle whose time has come.

Everything changes when we give ourselves permission to be more selective in what we choose to do. At once, we hold the key to unlock the next level of achievement in our lives. There is tremendous freedom in learning that we can eliminate the non-essentials, that we are no longer controlled by other people's agendas, and that we get to choose. With that invincible power we can discover our highest point of contribution, not just to our lives or careers, but to the world.

What if schools eliminated busywork and replaced it with important projects that made a difference to the whole community? What if all students had time to think about their highest contribution to their future so that when they left secondary school they were not just starting on the race to nowhere?[10]

What if businesses eliminated meaningless meetings and replaced them with space for people to think and work on their most important projects? What if employees pushed back against time-wasting e-mail chains, purposeless projects, and unproductive meetings so they could be utilised at their highest level of contribution to their companies and in their careers?

What if society stopped telling us to buy more stuff and instead allowed us to create more space to breathe and think? What if society encouraged us to reject what has been accurately described as doing things we detest, to buy things we don't need, with money we don't have, to impress people we don't like?[11]

What if we stopped being oversold the value of having more and being undersold the value of having less?

What if we stopped celebrating being busy as a measurement of importance? What if instead we celebrated how much time we had spent listening, pondering, meditating, and enjoying time with the most important people in our lives?

What if the whole world shifted from the undisciplined pursuit of more to the disciplined pursuit of less . . . only better?

I have a vision of people everywhere having the courage to live a life true to themselves instead of the life others expect of them.

I have a vision of everyone – children, students, mothers, fathers, employees, managers, executives, world leaders – learning to better tap into more of their intelligence, capability, resourcefulness, and initiative to live more meaningful lives. I have a vision of all these people courageously doing what they came here on this earth to do. I have a vision of starting a conversation that becomes a movement.

To harness the courage we need to get on the right path, it pays to reflect on how short life really is and what we want to accomplish in the little time we have left. As poet Mary Oliver wrote: "Tell me, what is it you plan to do / with your one wild and precious life?"[12]

I challenge you to pause more to ask yourself that question.

I challenge you here and now to make a commitment to make room to enjoy the essential. Do you think for one second you will regret such a decision? Is it at all likely you will wake up one day and say, "I wish I had been less true to myself and had done all the non-essential things others expected of me"?

I challenge you to let me help you to create a system that "unfairly" tips the scales in favour of the essential few over the trivial many.

I challenge you to invest in becoming more of an Essentialist. This book is not about going back to some simpler time. It's not about eschewing e-mail or disconnecting from the Web or living like a hermit. That would be backwards movement. It is about applying the principles of "less but better" to how we live our lives now and in the future. That is innovation.

So my challenge to you is to be wiser than I was on the day of my daughter's birth. I have great confidence in the good that can come from such a decision. Just imagine what would happen to our world if every person on the planet eliminated one good but non-essential activity and replaced it with something truly essential.

Years from now (hopefully many), when you are at the end of your life, you may still have regrets. But seeking the way of the Essentialist is unlikely to be one of them. What would you trade then to be back here now for one chance – this chance – to be true to yourself? On *that* day, what will you hope you decided to do on *this* one?

If you are ready to look inside yourself for the answer to this question, then you are ready to set out on the path of the Essentialist. Let us embark on it together.

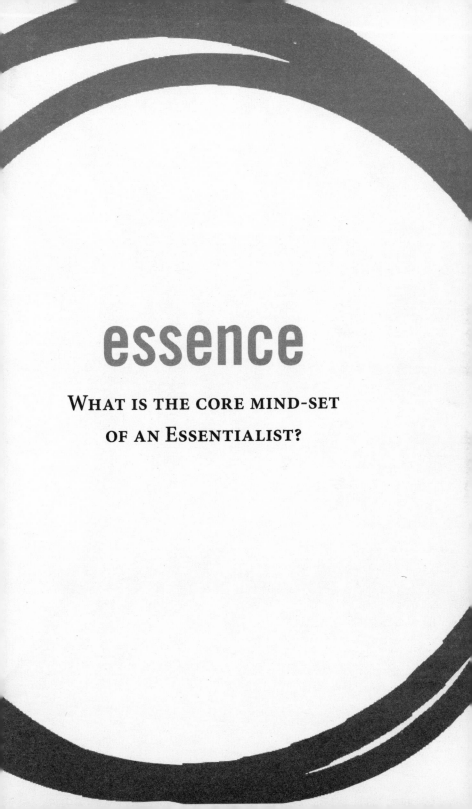

essence

WHAT IS THE CORE MIND-SET
OF AN ESSENTIALIST?

ESSENCE

What Is the Core Logic of an Essentialist?

Essentialism is not a way to do one more thing; it is a different way of doing everything. It is a way of thinking. But internalising this way of thinking is not a neutral challenge. This is because certain ideas – and people peddling those ideas – constantly pull us toward the logic of non-Essentialism. There are three chapters in this part of the book. Each takes on a fallacy of non-Essentialism and replaces it with a truth of Essentialism.

There are three deeply entrenched assumptions we must conquer to live the way of the Essentialist: "I have to," "It's all important," and "I can do both." Like mythological sirens, these assumptions are as dangerous as they are seductive. They draw us in and drown us in shallow waters.

To embrace the essence of Essentialism requires we replace these false assumptions with three core truths: "I choose to," "Only a few things really matter," and "I can do anything but not everything." These simple truths awaken us from our non-essential stupor. They free us to pursue what really matters. They enable us to live at our highest level of contribution.

As we rid ourselves of the nonsense of non-Essentialism and replace it with the core logic of Essentialism, the way of the Essentialist becomes natural and instinctive.

CHAPTER 2

CHOOSE

The Invincible Power of Choice

IT IS THE ABILITY TO CHOOSE WHICH MAKES US HUMAN.
—*Madeleine L'Engle*

I stared, wide-eyed, at the piece of paper in my hands. I was sitting in the foyer of a high-rise office building. It was dusk, and the last few people were trickling out for the evening. The piece of paper, covered with scribbled words and arrows, was the result of a twenty-minute spontaneous brainstorm about what I currently wanted to be doing with my life. As I looked at the paper I was mostly struck by what *wasn't* on it – law school was not on the list. This got my attention because I was halfway through my first year at law school in England.

I had applied to study law because of repeated advice to "keep your options open." Once I got out, I could practise law. I could write about law. I could teach law. Or I could consult on the law. The world would be my oyster, or so the argument went. Yet from almost the first moment I started studying law, instead of choosing between these pursuits I had simply tried to fit them all in. I would study my law books at all hours all day and read the great management thinkers in the evenings. In spare moments, I would write. It was a classic "straddled strategy" of attempting to invest in everything at once. The result was that while I was not entirely failing in any pursuit I was not entirely succeeding at any either. I soon began to wonder just what was so great about all these open options.

In the middle of all this existential confusion I received a call from a friend in the United States inviting me to his wedding. He had already bought and sent the tickets! So I gratefully accepted his invitation and left England for an unexpected adventure.

While in the United States I took every opportunity to meet teachers and writers. One such meeting was with an executive for a non-profit educational group. As I was leaving his office, he mentioned in passing, "If you decide to stay in America, you should come and join us on a consultation committee."

His passing comment had a curious force about it. It wasn't his specific question. It was the assumption he made that I had a choice: "*If* you decide to stay . . ." He saw it as a real option. This got me thinking.

I left his office and took the lift down to the lobby. I took a single sheet of paper from someone's desk and sat in the lobby and attempted to answer the question: "If you could do only one thing with your life right now, what would you do?"

The result was that piece of paper on which law school, as I have indicated, was not written.

Up to that point I had always known logically that I could choose not to study law. But *emotionally* it had never been an option. That's when I realised that in sacrificing my power to choose I *had* made a choice – a bad one. By refusing to choose "not law school," I had chosen law school – not because I actually or actively wanted to be there, but by default. I think that's when I first realised that when we surrender our ability to choose, something or someone else will step in to choose for us.

A few weeks later, I officially quit law school. I left England and moved to America to start down the path of becoming an author and a teacher. You're reading this now because of that choice.

Yet, for all the impact this specific choice has had on the trajectory of my life, I value the way it changed my view *about* choices even more. We often think of choice as a thing. But a choice is not a thing. Our options may be things, but a choice – a choice is an *action*. It is not just something we have but something we do. This experience brought me to the liberating realisation that while we may not always have control over our options, we *always* have control over how we choose among them.

Have you ever felt stuck because you believed you did not really have a choice? Have you ever felt the stress that comes from simultaneously holding two contradictory beliefs: "I can't do this" and "I have to do this"? Have you ever given up your power to choose bit by bit until you allowed yourself to blindly follow a path prescribed by another person?

If so, you are not alone.

The Invincible Power of Choosing to Choose

For too long, we have overemphasised the external aspect of choices (our options) and underemphasised our internal ability to choose (our actions). This is more than semantics. Think about it this way. Options (things) can be taken away, while our core ability to choose (free will) cannot be.

The ability to choose cannot be taken away or even given away – it can only be forgotten.

How Do We Forget Our Ability to Choose?

One important insight into how and why we forget our ability to choose comes out of the classic work of Martin Seligman and Steve Maier, who stumbled onto what they later called "learned helplessness" while conducting experiments on German shepherds.

Seligman and Maier divided the dogs into three groups. The dogs in the first group were placed in a harness and administered an electric shock but were also given a lever they could press to make the shock stop. The dogs in the second group were placed in an identical harness and were given the same lever, and the same shock, with one catch: the lever didn't work, rendering the dog powerless to do anything about the electric shock. The third group of dogs were simply placed in the harness and not given any shocks.[1]

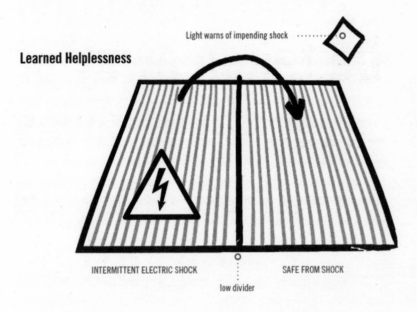

Learned Helplessness

Light warns of impending shock

INTERMITTENT ELECTRIC SHOCK   SAFE FROM SHOCK

low divider

Afterwards, each dog was placed in a large box with a low divider across the centre. One side of the box produced an electric shock; the other did not. Then something interesting happened. The dogs that either had been able to stop the shock or had not been shocked at all in the earlier part of the experiment quickly learned to step over the divider to the side without shocks. But the dogs that had been powerless in the last part of the experiment did not. These dogs didn't adapt or adjust. They did nothing to try to avoid getting shocked. Why? They didn't know they had any choice other than to take the shocks. They had learned helplessness.

There is evidence that humans learn helplessness in much the same way. One example I heard is that of a child who struggles early on with mathematics. He tries and tries but never gets any better, so eventually he gives up. He believes nothing he does will matter.

I have observed learned helplessness in many organisations I have worked with. When people believe that their efforts at work don't matter, they tend to respond in one of two ways. Sometimes they check out and stop trying, like the mathematically challenged child. The other response is less obvious at first. They do the opposite. They become hyperactive. They accept every opportunity presented. They throw themselves into every assignment. They tackle every challenge with gusto. They try to do it all. This behaviour does not necessarily look like learned helplessness at first glance. After all, isn't working hard evidence of one's belief in one's importance and value? Yet on closer examination we can see this compulsion to do more is a smokescreen. These people don't believe they have a choice in what opportunity, assignment, or challenge to take on. They believe they "have to do it all."

I'll be the first to admit that choices are hard. By definition they involve saying no to something or several somethings, and that can feel like a loss. Outside the workplace, choices can be even harder. Any time we walk into a store or a restaurant or anywhere selling something, everything is designed to make it hard for us to say no. When we listen to a political advertisement or pundit, the objective is to make it unthinkable for us to vote for the other side. When our mother-in-law calls us up (mine excluded of course) and wants us to do something, it can be hardest of all to feel we really have a choice. If we look at everyday life through this lens, it is hardly surprising we forget our ability to choose.

Yet choice is at the very core of what it means to be an Essentialist. To become an Essentialist requires a heightened awareness of our ability to choose. We need to recognise it as an invincible power within us, existing separate and distinct from any other thing, person, or force. William James once wrote, "My first act of free will shall be to believe in free will."[2] That is why the first and most crucial skill you will learn on this journey is to develop your ability to choose choice, in every area of your life.

Non-Essentialist	Essentialist
"I have to."	"I choose to."
Forfeits the right to choose	Exercises the power of choice

When we forget our ability to choose, we learn to be helpless. Drip by drip we allow our power to be taken away until we end up becoming a function of other people's choices – or even a function of our own past choices. In turn, we surrender our power to choose. That is the path of the non-Essentialist.

The Essentialist doesn't just recognise the power of choice, he celebrates it. The Essentialist knows that when we surrender our right to choose, we give others not just the power but also the explicit permission to choose for us.

Chapter 3

DISCERN

The Unimportance of Practically Everything

MOST OF WHAT EXISTS IN THE UNIVERSE – OUR
ACTIONS, AND ALL OTHER FORCES, RESOURCES,
AND IDEAS – HAS LITTLE VALUE AND YIELDS LITTLE
RESULT; ON THE OTHER HAND, A FEW THINGS WORK
FANTASTICALLY WELL AND HAVE TREMENDOUS IMPACT.

—*Richard Koch*

In George Orwell's classic allegorical novel *Animal Farm* we are introduced to the fictional character Boxer the horse. He is described as faithful and strong. His answer to every setback and every problem is, "I will work harder." He lives true to his philosophy under the direst circumstances until, exhausted and broken, he is sent to the knackers' yard. He is a tragic figure: despite his best intentions, his ever-increasing efforts actually exacerbate the inequality and problems on the farm.

Are there ways we can be a bit like Boxer? Do setbacks often only strengthen our resolve to work longer and harder? Do we sometimes respond to every challenge with "Yes, I can take this on as well"? After all, we have been taught from a young age that hard work is key to producing results, and many of us have been amply rewarded for our productivity and our ability to muscle through every task or challenge the world throws at us. Yet, for capable people who are already working hard, are there limits to the value of hard work? Is there a point at which doing more does *not* produce more? Is there a point at which doing *less* (but thinking more) will actually produce better outcomes?

I remember when I was young I wanted to earn some pocket money. One of the few jobs available for twelve-year-olds in England was a paper round. It paid about a pound a day and took about an hour. So for a while I heaved a bag that seemed heavier than I was from door to door for an hour each morning before school (and just for the record, we couldn't just throw the paper onto someone's front porch, as is done in the United States. We had to take the paper up to the tiny letterbox on the door and then force the paper all the way through it). It was hard-earned pocket money, to be sure.

The considerable effort I had to put in just to earn that one pound a day forever changed the way I thought about the cost of the things I desired. From then on, when I looked at something I wanted to buy I would translate it into the number of days I would have to deliver the papers to get it. One pound of reward equalled one hour of effort. I realised that at this rate it would take quite a while to save up for that MicroMachine I wanted.

Then, as I started to think about how I might speed up the process, I had the insight that I could clean the neighbours' cars on Saturday mornings instead of delivering papers. I could charge two pounds per car and could clean three in an hour. Suddenly, the ratio of hours to pounds changed from 1:1 to 1:6. I had just learned a crucial lesson: certain types of effort yield higher rewards than others.

Years later at university I went to work for a coaching company. I worked in their customer service department for $9 an hour. It would have been easy to think of the jobs in terms of that ratio between time and reward. But I knew what really counted was the relationship between time and *results*.

So I asked myself, "What is the most valuable result I could achieve in this job?" It turned out to be winning back customers who wanted to cancel. So I worked hard at convincing customers not to cancel, and soon I achieved a zero rate of cancellation. Since I was paid for each client I retained, I learned more, earned more, and contributed more.

Working hard is important. But more effort does not necessarily yield more results. "Less but better" does.

Ferran Adrià, arguably the world's greatest chef, who has led El Bulli to become the world's most famous restaurant, epitomises the principle of "less but better" in at least two ways. First, his speciality is reducing traditional dishes to their absolute essence and then reimagining them in ways people have never thought of before. Second, while El Bulli has somewhere in the range of 2 million requests for dinner reservations each year, it serves only fifty people per night and closes for six months of the year. In fact, at the time of writing, Ferran had stopped serving food altogether and had instead turned El Bulli into a full-time food laboratory of sorts where he was continuing to pursue nothing but the essence of his craft.[1]

Getting used to the idea of "less but better" may prove harder than it sounds, especially when we have been rewarded in the past for doing more . . . and more and more. Yet at a certain point, more effort causes our progress to plateau and even stall. It's true that the idea of a direct correlation between results and effort is appealing. It seems fair. Yet research across many fields paints a very different picture.

Most people have heard of the "Pareto Principle," the idea, introduced as far back as the 1790s by Vilfredo Pareto, that 20 per cent of our efforts produce 80 per cent of results. Much later, in

1951, in his *Quality-Control Handbook,* Joseph Moses Juran, one of the fathers of the quality movement, expanded on this idea and called it "the Law of the Vital Few."[2] His observation was that you could massively improve the quality of a product by resolving a tiny fraction of the problems. He found a willing test audience for this idea in Japan, which at the time had developed a rather poor reputation for producing low-cost, low-quality goods. By adopting a process in which a high percentage of effort and attention was channelled towards improving just those few things that were truly vital, he made the phrase "made in Japan" take on a totally new meaning. And gradually, the quality revolution led to Japan's rise as a global economic power.[3]

Distinguishing the "trivial many" from the "vital few" can be applied to every kind of human endeavour large or small and has been done so persuasively by Richard Koch, author of several books on how to apply the Pareto Principle (80/20 Rule) to everyday life.[4] Indeed, the examples are everywhere.

Think of Warren Buffett, who has famously said, "Our investment philosophy borders on lethargy."[5] What he means is that he and his firm make relatively few investments and keep them for a long time. In *The Tao of Warren Buffett,* Mary Buffett and David Clark explain: "Warren decided early in his career it would be impossible for him to make hundreds of right investment decisions, so he decided that he would invest only in the businesses that he was absolutely sure of, and then bet heavily on them. He owes 90% of his wealth to just ten investments. Sometimes what you don't do is just as important as what you do."[6] In short, he makes big bets on the essential few investment opportunities and says no to the many merely good ones.[7]

Some believe the relationship between efforts and results is even less linear, following what scientists call a "power law." According to the power law theory, certain efforts actually produce exponentially more results than others. For example, as Nathan Myhrvold, the former chief technology officer for Microsoft, has said (and then confirmed to me in person), "The top software developers are more productive than average software developers not by a factor of 10X or 100X or even 1,000X but by 10,000X."[8] It may be an exaggeration, but it still makes the point that *certain* efforts produce exponentially better results than others.

The overwhelming reality is: we live in a world where almost everything is worthless and a very few things are exceptionally valuable. As John Maxwell has written, "You cannot overestimate the unimportance of practically everything."[9]

A non-Essentialist thinks almost everything is essential.

An Essentialist thinks almost everything is non-essential.

As we unlearn the 1:1 logic, we begin to see the value in pursuing the way of the Essentialist. We discover how even the many good opportunities we pursue are often far less valuable than the few truly great ones. Once we understand this, we start scanning our environment for those vital few and eagerly eliminate the trivial many. Only then can we say no to good opportunities and say yes to truly great ones.

This is why an Essentialist takes the time to explore all his options. The extra investment is justified because some things are *so* much more important that they repay the effort invested in finding those things tenfold. An Essentialist, in other words, discerns more so he can *do* less.

Non-Essentialist	Essentialist
Thinks almost everything is essential	Thinks almost everything is non-essential
Views opportunities as basically equal	Distinguishes the vital few from the trivial many

Many capable people are kept from getting to the next level of contribution because they can't let go of the belief that everything is important. But an Essentialist has learned to tell the difference between what is truly important and everything else. To practise this Essentialist skill we can start at a simple level, and once it becomes second nature for everyday decisions we can begin to apply it to bigger and broader areas of our personal and professional lives. To master it fully will require a massive shift in thinking. But it can be done.

Chapter 4

TRADE-OFF

Which Problem Do I Want?

STRATEGY IS ABOUT MAKING CHOICES, TRADE-OFFS.
IT'S ABOUT DELIBERATELY CHOOSING TO BE DIFFERENT.

—*Michael Porter*

Imagine you could go back to 1972 and invest a dollar in each company in the S&P 500. Which company would provide the largest return on your investment by 2002? Would it be GE? IBM? Intel? According to *Money* magazine and the analysis they initiated from Ned Davis Research, the answer is none of the above.[1]

The correct answer is Southwest Airlines. This is startling because the airline industry is notoriously bad at generating profits. Yet Southwest, led by Herb Kelleher, has consistently, year after year, produced amazing financial results. Herb's Essentialist approach to business is central to why.

I once attended an event where Herb was interviewed about his business strategy.[2] It was a great talk in many ways, but when he began to talk about how deliberate he was about the trade-offs he had made at Southwest, my ears perked up. Rather than try to fly to every destination, they had deliberately chosen to offer only point-to-point flights. Instead of jacking up prices to cover the cost of meals, he decided they would serve none. Instead of assigning seats in advance, they would let people choose them as they got on the plane. Instead of upselling their passengers on glitzy first-class service, they offered only economy. These trade-offs weren't made by default but by design. Each and every one was made as part of a deliberate strategy to keep costs down. Did he run the risk of alienating customers who wanted the broader range of destinations, the choice to purchase overpriced meals, and so forth? Yes, but Kelleher was totally clear about what the company was – a low-cost airline – and what they were not. And his trade-offs reflected as much.

It was an example of his Essentialist thinking at work when he said: "You have to look at every opportunity and say, 'Well, no . . . I'm sorry. We're not going to do a thousand different things that really won't contribute much to the end result we are trying to achieve.'"

At first, Southwest was lambasted by critics, naysayers, and other non-Essentialists who couldn't believe that this approach could possibly be successful. Who in their right mind would want to fly with an airline that travelled only to certain places and didn't serve meals, no matter how cheap tickets were? Yet after a few years it became clear Southwest was onto something. Competitors in the industry took notice of Southwest's soaring profits and started trying to imitate their approach. But instead of adopting Kelleher's Essentialist approach carte blanche, they did what Harvard Business School professor Michel Porter terms "straddling" their strategy.

In the simplest terms, *straddling* means keeping your existing strategy intact while simultaneously also trying to adopt the strategy of a competitor. One of the most visible attempts at the time was made by Continental Airlines. They called their new point-to-point service Continental Lite.

Continental Lite adopted some of Southwest's practices. They lowered their fares. They got rid of meals. They stopped their first-class service. They increased the frequency of departures. The problem was that because they were still hanging onto their existing business model (Continental Lite accounted for only a small percentage of flights offered by the airline) they didn't have the operational efficiencies that would allow them to compete on price. So they were forced to skimp in other ways that ended up compromising the quality of their service. While Southwest had made conscious, deliberate trade-offs in key strategic areas, Continental was forced to sacrifice things around the margins that weren't part of a coherent strategy. According to Porter, "A strategic position is not sustainable unless there are trade-offs with other positions."[3] By trying to operate by two incompatible strategies they started to undermine their ability to be competitive.

The straddled strategy was enormously expensive for Continental. They lost hundreds of millions of dollars to delayed planes, and, according to Porter, "late flights and cancellations generated a thousand complaints a day." The CEO was eventually fired. The moral of the story: *ignoring the reality of trade-offs is a terrible strategy for organisations.* It turns out to be a terrible strategy for people as well.

Have you ever spent time with someone who is always trying to fit just one more thing in? Such people know they have ten minutes to get to a meeting that takes ten minutes to walk to, but they still sit down to answer a couple of e-mails before they go. Or they agree to put together a report by Friday, even though they have another huge deadline that same day. Or maybe they promise to swing by their cousin's birthday party on Saturday night, even though they already have tickets to a show that starts at exactly the same time. Their logic, which ignores the reality of trade-offs, is *I can do both.* The rather important problem is that this logic is false. Inevitably, they are late to the meeting, they miss one or both of their deadlines (or do a shoddy job on both projects), and they either don't make it to their cousin's celebration or miss the show. The reality is, saying yes to any opportunity by definition requires saying no to several others.

Trade-offs are real, in both our personal and our professional lives, and until we accept that reality we'll be doomed to be just like Continental – stuck in a "straddled strategy" that forces us to make sacrifices on the margins by default that we might not have made by design.

In an insightful opinion piece for the *New York Times,* Erin Callan, the former CFO of Lehman Brothers, shared what she had sacrificed in making trade-offs by default. She wrote: "I didn't start out with the goal of devoting all of myself to my job. It crept in over time. Each year that went by, slight modifications became the new normal. First I spent a half-hour on Sunday organizing my e-mail, to-do list, and calendar to make Monday morning easier. Then I was working a few hours on Sunday, then all day. My boundaries slipped away until work was all that was left."[4] Her story demonstrates a critical truth: we can either make the hard choices for ourselves or allow others – whether our colleagues, our boss, or our customers – to decide for us.

In my work I've noticed that senior executives of companies are among the worst at accepting the reality of trade-offs. I recently spent some time with the CEO of a company in Silicon Valley valued at $40 billion. He shared with me the value statement of his organisation, which he had just crafted, and which he planned to announce to the whole company. But when he shared it I cringed: "We value passion, innovation, execution, and leadership."

One of several problems with the list is, Who *doesn't* value these things? Another problem is that this tells employees nothing about what the company values *most*. It says nothing about what choices employees should be making when these values are at odds. This is similarly true when companies claim that their mission is to serve all stakeholders – clients, employees, shareholders – equally. To say they value equally everyone they interact with leaves management with no clear guidance on what to do when faced with trade-offs between the people they serve.

Contrast this with how Johnson & Johnson bounced back from the tragic cyanide murder scandal in 1982.[5] At the time Johnson & Johnson owned 37 per cent of the market and Tylenol was their most profitable product. Then reports surfaced that seven people had died after taking Tylenol. It was later discovered that these bottles had been tampered with. How should Johnson & Johnson respond?

The question was a complicated one. Was their primary responsibility to ensure the safety of their customers by immediately taking all Tylenol products off chemist's shelves? Was their first priority to do PR damage control to keep shareholders from dumping their stock? Or was it their duty to console and compensate the families of the victims first and foremost?

Fortunately for them they had the Credo: a statement written in 1943 by then chairman Robert Wood Johnson that is literally carved in stone at Johnson & Johnson headquarters.[6] Unlike most corporate mission statements, the Credo actually lists the constituents of the company in priority order. Customers are first; shareholders are last.

As a result, Johnson & Johnson swiftly decided to recall all

Tylenol, even though it would have a massive impact (to the tune of $100 million, according to some reports) on their bottom line. The safety of customers *or* $100 million? Not an easy decision. But the Credo enabled a clearer sense of what was most essential. It enabled the tough trade-off to be made.

We can try to avoid the reality of trade-offs, but we can't escape them.

I once worked with an executive team that needed help with their prioritisation. They were struggling to identify the top five projects they wanted their IT department to complete over the next fiscal year, and one of the managers was having a particularly hard time with it. She insisted on naming *eighteen* "top priority" projects. I insisted that she choose five. She took her list back to her team, and two weeks later they returned with a list she had managed to shorten – by *one* single project! (I always wondered what it was about that one lone project that didn't make the cut.) By refusing to make trade-offs, she ended up spreading five projects' worth of time and effort across seventeen projects. Unsurprisingly, she did not get the results she wanted. Her logic had been: *We can do it all*. Obviously not.

It is easy to see why it's so tempting to deny the reality of trade-offs. After all, by definition, a trade-off involves two things we want. Do you want more pay or more holiday time? Do you want to finish this next e-mail or be on time to your meeting? Do you want it done faster or better? Obviously, when faced with the choice between two things we want, the preferred answer is *yes* to both. But as much as we'd like to, we simply cannot have it all.

A non-Essentialist approaches every trade-off by asking, "How can I do both?" Essentialists ask the tougher but ultimately more liberating question, "Which problem do I want?" An Essentialist makes trade-offs deliberately. She acts for herself rather than waiting to be acted upon. As economist Thomas Sowell wrote: "There are no solutions. There are only trade-offs."[7]

Jim Collins, the author of the business classic *Good to Great*, was once told by Peter Drucker that he could either build a great company or build great ideas but not both. Jim chose ideas. As a result of this trade-off there are still only three full-time employees in his company, yet his ideas have reached tens of millions of people through his writing.[8]

As painful as they can sometimes be, trade-offs represent a significant opportunity. By forcing us to weigh both options and strategically select the best one for us, we significantly increase our chance of achieving the outcome *we* want. Like Southwest, we can enjoy the success that results from making a consistent set of choices.

I observed an example of this on a recent flight to Boston, when I began chatting with two parents who were on their way to visit their son at Harvard. They were clearly proud their son was there, and I was curious about what strategy they and he had pursued in getting him accepted. They said, "We had him try out a lot of different things, but as soon as it became clear an activity was not going to be his 'big thing' we discussed it and took him out of it." The point here is not that all parents should want their children to go to Harvard. The point is that these Essentialist parents had consciously decided their goal was for their son to go to Harvard and understood that that success required making strategic trade-offs.

This logic holds true in our personal lives as well. When we were newlyweds, Anna and I met someone who had, as far as we could tell, an amazing marriage and family. We wanted to learn from him, so we asked him, *What's your secret*? One of the things he told us was that he and his wife had decided not to be a part of any clubs. He didn't join the local golf club. She didn't join the book clubs. It wasn't that they had no interest in those things. It was simply that they made the trade-off to spend that time with their children. Over the years their children had become their best friends – well worth the sacrifice of any friendships they might have made on the golf course or over tattered copies of *Anna Karenina*.

Essentialists see trade-offs as an inherent part of life, not as an inherently negative part of life. Instead of asking, "What do I have to give up?" they ask, "What do I want to go big on?" The cumulative impact of this small change in thinking can be profound.

Non-Essentialist	Essentialist
Thinks, "I can do both." Asks, "How can I do it all?"	Asks, "What is the trade-off I want to make?" Asks, "What can I go big on?"

In a piece called "Laugh, Kookaburra" published in *The New Yorker,* David Sedaris gives a humorous account of his experience touring the Australian "bush."[9] While hiking, his friend and guide for the day shares something she has heard in passing at a management class. "Imagine a four-burner stove," she instructs the members of the party. "One burner represents your family, one is your friends, the third is your health, and the fourth is your work. In order to be successful you have to cut off one of your burners. And in order to be really successful you have to cut off two."

Of course, this was tongue-in-cheek; I am not here to suggest that living the way of the Essentialist requires us to decide between our families and our health and our work. What I am suggesting is that when faced with a decision where one option prioritises family and another prioritises friends, health, or work, we need to be prepared to ask, "Which problem do you want?"

Trade-offs are not something to be ignored or decried. They are something to be embraced and made deliberately, strategically, and thoughtfully.

explore

How can we discern the trivial many from the vital few?

EXPLORE

Discern the Vital Few from the Trivial Many

One paradox of Essentialism is that Essentialists actually explore *more* options than their non-Essentialist counterparts. Non-Essentialists get excited by virtually everything and thus react to everything. But because they are so busy pursuing every opportunity and idea they actually explore *less*. The way of the Essentialist, on the other hand, is to explore and evaluate a broad set of options before committing to any. Because Essentialists will commit and "go big" on only the vital few ideas or activities, they explore more options at first to ensure they pick the right one later.

In Part Two, we will discuss five practices for exploring what is essential. The gravitational pull of non-Essentialism can be so strong that it can be tempting to skip over or skim over this step. Yet this step, in itself, is essential to the disciplined pursuit of less. To discern what is truly essential we need space to think, time to look and listen, permission to play, wisdom to sleep, and the discipline to apply highly selective criteria to the choices we make.

Ironically, in a non-Essentialist culture these things — space, listening, playing, sleeping, and selecting — can be seen *as* trivial distractions. At best they are considered nice to have. At worst they are derided as evidence of weakness and wastefulness. We all know that highly ambitious or productive person who thinks, "Of course, I'd love to be able to set aside time on the calendar simply to think, but it's a luxury we can't afford right now." Or "Play? Who has time for play? We are here to work!" or as one leader said to me in an induction process, "I hope you had a good night's sleep. You won't get much of that here."

If you believe being overly busy and overextended is evidence of productivity, then you probably believe that creating space to explore, think, and reflect should be kept to a minimum. Yet these very activities are the antidote to the nonessential busyness that infects so many of us. Rather than trivial diversions, they are critical to distinguishing what *is* actually a trivial diversion from what *is* truly essential.

Essentialists spend as much time as possible exploring, listening, debating, questioning, and thinking. But their exploration is not an end in itself. The purpose of the exploration is to discern the vital few from the trivial many.

CHAPTER 5

ESCAPE

The Perks of Being Unavailable

WITHOUT GREAT SOLITUDE NO SERIOUS
WORK IS POSSIBLE.

—*Pablo Picasso*

Frank O'Brien is the founder of Conversations, a marketing services company based in New York that has been named on the Inc. 500/5000 List of "America's Fastest Growing Private Companies." In response to the frenetic pace of today's workplace he has initiated a radical practice.

Once a month he gathers each employee of his fifty-person company into a room for a full day. Phones are prohibited. E-mail is outlawed. There is no agenda. The purpose of the meeting is simply to escape to think and to talk. Mind you, he doesn't hold this meeting on the middle Friday of the month, when productivity might be sluggish and people aren't getting any "real work" done anyway. He holds this daylong meeting on the first Monday of the month. The practice isn't just an internal discipline either: even his clients know not to expect a response on this "Do-Not-Call-Monday."[1]

He does this because he knows his people can't figure out what is essential if they're constantly on call. They need space to figure out what really matters. He wrote: "I think it's critical to set aside time to take a breath, look around, and think. You need that level of clarity in order to innovate and grow." Furthermore, he uses the meeting as a litmus test to alert him if employees are spending too much time on the non-essential: "If somebody can't make the meeting because of too much going on, that tells me either we're doing something inefficiently or we need to hire more people." If his people are too busy to think, then they're too busy, period.

We need space to escape in order to discern the essential few from the trivial many. Unfortunately, in our time-starved era we don't get that space by default – only by design. One leader I worked with admitted to staying with a company five years too long. Why? Because he was so busy *in* the company he didn't take time to decide whether he should be *with* the company. The demands of each day kept him from really stepping back to get perspective.

Similarly, a senior vice president at a major global technology company told me he spends thirty-five hours every week in meetings. He is so consumed with these meetings he cannot find even an hour a month to strategise about his own career, let alone how to take his organisation to the next level. Instead of giving himself the space to talk and debate what is really going on and what really needs to happen, he squanders his time sitting through endless presentations and stuffy, cross-functional conversations where nothing is really decided.

Before you can evaluate what is and isn't essential, you first need to explore your options. While non-Essentialists automatically react to the latest idea, jump on the latest opportunity, or respond to the latest e-mail, Essentialists choose to create the space to explore and ponder.

Non-Essentialist	Essentialist
Is too busy doing to think about life	Creates space to escape and explore life

Space to Design

The value of creating space to explore has been emphasised for me in my work with the d.school at Stanford (officially the Hasso Plattner Institute of Design at Stanford). The first thing I noticed when I walked into the room where I had been asked to teach a course was the lack of traditional chairs. Instead there are foam cubes you can sit on – rather uncomfortably, as I soon discovered. Like almost everything at the d.school, this is done by design. In this case the cubes are there so that after a few minutes of uncomfortable perching students would *rather* stand up, walk around, and engage with one another – not just the classmates sitting to their right or to their left. And that is the point. The school has used the physical space to encourage new ways of engaging and thinking.

To that end, the school has also created a hiding place called "Booth Noir." This is a small room deliberately designed to fit only one to three people. It is windowless, soundproof, and deliberately free of distraction. It is, according to Scott Doorley and Scott Witthoft in their book *Make Space,* "beyond low-tech. It's no tech." It's tucked away on the ground floor. It is not, as Doorley and Witthoft point out, on the way to anywhere else.[2] The only reason you go there is to think. By creating space to think and focus, students can step back to see more clearly.

For some reason there is a false association with the word *focus.* As with choice, people tend to think of focus as a thing. Yes, focus is something we have. But focus is also something we *do.*

In order to *have* focus we need to escape *to* focus.

When I say *focus*, I don't mean simply picking a question or possibility and thinking about it obsessively. I mean creating the space to explore one hundred questions and possibilities. An Essentialist focuses the way our eyes focus; not by fixating on something but by constantly adjusting and adapting to the field of vision.

On a recent meeting back at the d.school (in another room with no seats or desks but with whiteboards from floor to ceiling covered with Post-its of every fathomable colour), I met with Jeremy Utley. He is my partner in developing a new prototyped class that, in a moment of genius, Jeremy dubbed "Designing Life, Essentially."

The sole purpose of the class is to create space for students to design their lives. Each week it gives them a scheduled excuse to think. They are forced to turn off their laptops and smartphones and instead to turn on the full power of their minds. They are given assignments to practise deliberately discerning the essential few from the many good. You don't have to be at the d.school to practise these habits. We can all learn to create more space in our lives.

Space to Concentrate

One executive I know is intelligent and driven but constantly distracted. At any given time he will have Twitter, Gmail, Facebook, and multiple IM conversations going at once. In an effort to create a distraction-free space, he once tried getting his executive assistant to pull all of the Internet cables out of his computer. But he still found too many ways to get online. So, when he was struggling to complete a particularly big project, he resorted to a desperate measure. He gave his phone away and went to a motel with no Internet access. After eight weeks of almost solitary confinement, he was able to get the project done.

To me, it is a little sad that this executive was driven to such measures. Yet while his methods may have been extreme, I can't argue with his intention. He knew that making his highest point of contribution on a task required that he create the space for unencumbered thought.

Think of Sir Isaac Newton. He spent two years working on what became *Principia Mathematica,* his famous writings on universal gravitation and the three laws of motion. This period of almost solitary confinement proved critical in what became a true breakthrough that shaped scientific thinking for the next three hundred years.

Richard S. Westfall has written: "In the age of his celebrity, Newton was asked how he had discovered the law of universal gravitation. 'By thinking on it continually' was the reply.... What he thought on, he thought on continually, which is to say exclusively, or nearly exclusively."[3] In other words, Newton created space for intense concentration, and this uninterrupted space enabled him to explore the essential elements of the universe.

Inspired by Newton, I took a similar, if perhaps less extreme, approach to writing this book. I blocked off eight hours a day to write: from 5 a.m. to 1 p.m., five days a week. The basic rule was no e-mail, no calls, no appointments, and no interruptions until after 1 p.m. I didn't always achieve it, but the discipline made a big difference. I set my e-mail automatic replies to explain that I was in "monk mode" until after the book was complete. It is difficult to overstate how much freedom I found in this approach. By creating space to explore, think, and write, I not only got my book done faster but gained control over how I spent the rest of my time.

It seems obvious, but when did you last take time out of your busy day simply to sit and think? I don't mean the five minutes during your morning commute you spent composing the day's to-do list, or the meeting you spent zoned out reflecting on how to approach another project you were working on. I'm talking about deliberately setting aside distraction-free time in a distraction-free space to do absolutely nothing other than think.

This is of course more difficult today than ever in our gadget-filled, overstimulated world. One leader at Twitter once asked me: "Can you remember what it was like to be bored? It doesn't happen anymore." He's right; just a few years ago if you were stuck in an airport waiting for a delayed flight, or in the waiting room of a doctor's surgery, you probably just sat there, staring into space, feeling bored. Today, everyone waiting around in an airport or a waiting room is glued to their technology tools of choice. Of course, nobody likes to be bored. But by abolishing any chance of being bored we have also lost the time we used to have to think and process.

Here's another paradox for you: the faster and busier things get, the more we need to build thinking time into our schedule. And the noisier things get, the more we need to build quiet reflection spaces in which we can truly focus.

No matter how busy you think you are, you *can* carve time and space to think out of your workday. Jeff Weiner, the CEO of LinkedIn, for example, schedules up to two hours of blank space on his calendar every day. He divides them into thirty-minute increments, yet he schedules nothing. It is a simple practice he developed when back-to-back meetings left him with little time to process what was going on around him.[4] At first it felt like an indulgence, a waste of time. But eventually he found it to be his single most valuable productivity tool. He sees it as the primary way he can ensure *he* is in charge of his own day, instead of being at the mercy of it.

As he explained to me: "I do recall one particular day where, by virtue of circumstances, I was either on conference calls or in meetings non-stop from 5 a.m. until 9 p.m. At the end of the day, I remember how frustrated I felt by the thought that I was not in control of my schedule that day; rather, it was in control of me. However, that frustration immediately gave way to a sense of gratitude given it was the only day I could recall feeling like that since taking my current role."

In this space he is able to think about the essential questions: what the company will look like in three to five years; what's the best way to improve an already popular product or address an unmet customer need; how to widen a competitive advantage or close a competitive gap. He also uses the space he creates to recharge himself emotionally. This allows him to shift between problem-solving mode and the coaching mode expected of him as a leader.

For Jeff creating space is more than a practice. It is part of a broader philosophy. He has seen the effects of the undisciplined pursuit of more on organisations and in the lives of executives. So for him it's not a slogan or a buzz phrase. It is a philosophy.

Space to Read

We can take further inspiration from the example of CEO Bill Gates, who regularly (and famously) takes a regular week off from his daily duties at Microsoft simply to think and read. I once attended a question-and-answer session with Bill at the headquarters of the Bill and Melinda Gates Foundation in Seattle, Washington. By chance he had just completed his latest "Think Week." Though I had heard about this practice, what I didn't know was that it goes all the way back to the 1980s and that he stuck to it through the height of Microsoft's expansion.[5]

In other words, twice a year, during the busiest and most frenetic time in the company's history, he still created time and space to seclude himself for a week and do nothing but read articles (his record is 112) and books, study technology, and think about the bigger picture. Today he still takes the time away from the daily distractions of running his foundation to simply think.

If setting aside a full week seems overwhelming or impossible, there are ways of putting a little "Think Week" into every day. One practice I've found useful is simply to read something from classic literature (not a blog, or the newspaper, or the latest beach novel) for the first twenty minutes of the day. Not only does this squash my previous tendency to check my e-mail as soon as I wake up, it centres my day. It broadens my perspective and reminds me of themes and ideas that are essential enough to have withstood the test of time.

My preference is for inspirational literature, though such a choice is a personal one. But for the interested, here are some to consider: *Zen, the Reason of Unreason; The Wisdom of Confucius;* the Torah; the Holy Bible; *Tao, to Know and Not Be Knowing; The Meaning of the Glorious Koran: An Explanatory Translation; As a Man Thinketh; The Essential Gandhi; Walden, or, Life in the Woods;*

the Book of Mormon; *The Meditations of Marcus Aurelius;* and the Upanishads. There are a myriad of options. Just make sure you select something that was written before our hyperconnected era and yet seems timeless. Such writings can challenge our assumptions about what really matters.

Whether you can invest two hours a day, two weeks a year, or even just five minutes every morning, it is important to make space to escape in your busy life.

Chapter 6

LOOK

See What Really Matters

WHERE IS THE KNOWLEDGE WE HAVE
LOST IN INFORMATION?

– T. S. Eliot

The late writer Nora Ephron is arguably best known for movies like *Silkwood, Sleepless in Seattle,* and *When Harry Met Sally,* each of which was nominated for an Academy Award. Ephron's success as a writer and screenwriter has a lot to do with her ability to capture the *essence* of a story – a skill she honed in her earlier career as a journalist. But for all her years in the high-octane world of journalism, the lesson that affected her most profoundly dates all the way back to her high school years.

Charlie O. Simms taught a Journalism 101 class at Beverly Hills High School. He started the first day of the class Ephron attended much the same way any journalism teacher would, by explaining the concept of a "lead." He explained that a lead contains the *why, what, when,* and *who* of the piece. It covers the essential information. Then he gave them their first assignment: write a lead to a story.

Simms began by presenting the facts of the story: "Kenneth L. Peters, the principal of Beverly Hills High School, announced today that the entire high school faculty will travel to Sacramento next Thursday for a colloquium in new teaching methods. Among the speakers will be anthropologist Margaret Mead, college president Dr. Robert Maynard Hutchins, and California governor Edmund 'Pat' Brown."

The students hammered away on their manual typewriters trying to keep up with the teacher's pace. Then they handed in their rapidly written leads. Each attempted to summarise the who, what, where, and why as succinctly as possible: "Margaret Mead, Maynard Hutchins, and Governor Brown will address the faculty on . . ."; "Next Thursday, the high school faculty will . . ." Simms reviewed the students' leads and put them aside.

He then informed them that they were all wrong. The lead to the story, he said, was "There will be no school Thursday."

"In that instant," Ephron recalled, "I realised that journalism was not just about regurgitating the facts but about figuring out the *point*. It wasn't enough to know the who, what, when, and where; you had to understand what it meant. And why it mattered." Ephron added, "He taught me something that works just as well in life as it does in journalism."[1]

In every set of facts, something essential is hidden. And a good journalist knows that finding it involves exploring those pieces of information and figuring out the relationships between them (and my undergraduate degree was in journalism, so I take this seriously). It means making those relationships and connections explicit. It means constructing the whole from the sum of its parts and understanding how these different pieces come together to matter to anyone. The best journalists do not simply relay information. Their value is in discovering what really matters to people.

Have you ever felt lost and unsure about what to focus on? Have you ever felt overwhelmed by all of the information bombarding you and not sure what to make of it? Have you ever felt dizzy from the different requests coming at you and unable to figure out which are important and which are not? Have you ever missed the point of something in your work or at home and not realised your mistake until it was too late? If so, this next Essentialist skill will be immensely valuable.

The Big Picture

On 29 December, 1972, Eastern Air Lines Flight 401 crashed into the Florida Everglades, killing over one hundred passengers.[2] It was the first-ever crash of a wide-body aircraft and one of the worst airline crashes in US history. The investigators were later shocked to discover that, in all vital ways, the plane had been in perfect working condition. So what went wrong?

The Lockheed jet had been preparing to land when first officer Albert Stockstill noticed that the landing gear indicator, a tiny green light that signals the nose gear is locked down, hadn't lit up. Yet the nose gear was locked; the problem was the indicator light, not the gear function. While the officers were hyperfocused on the gear indicator, however, they failed to notice that the autopilot had been deactivated until it was too late. In other words, the nose gear didn't cause the disaster. The crew's losing sight of the bigger problem – the altitude of the plane – did.

Being a journalist of your own life will force you to stop hyperfocusing on all the minor details and see the bigger picture. You can apply the skills of a journalist no matter what field you are in – you can even apply them to your personal life. By training yourself to look for "the lead," you will suddenly find yourself able to see what you have missed. You'll be able to do more than simply see the dots of each day: you'll also connect them to see the trends. Instead of just reacting to the facts, you'll be able to focus on the larger issues that really matter.

Filter for the Fascinating

We know instinctively that we cannot explore every single piece of information we encounter in our lives. Discerning what *is* essential to explore requires us to be disciplined in how we scan and filter all the competing and conflicting facts, options, and opinions constantly vying for our attention.

Recently, I chatted with Thomas Friedman, the *New York Times* columnist and award-winning journalist, about how to filter the essential information from the non-essential noise. Before I met him he had been at a lunch meeting with sources for a column he was writing. Someone at lunch thought at first that he was not paying attention to the banter at the table. But he *was* listening. He was taking in the whole conversation at the table. He was simply filtering out everything other than those things that really grabbed his attention. Then he tried to connect the dots by asking lots of questions only about what had just piqued his interest.

The best journalists, as Friedman shared later with me, listen for what others do not hear. At the lunch, he had been listening for what was being said only at the periphery. He was listening more for what was *not* being said.

Essentialists are powerful observers and listeners. Knowing that the reality of trade-offs means they can't possibly pay attention to everything, they listen deliberately for what is not being explicitly stated. They read between the lines. Or as Hermione Granger, of *Harry Potter* fame (an unlikely Essentialist, I'll grant you, but an Essentialist in this regard all the same), puts it, "Actually I'm highly logical, which allows me to look past extraneous detail and perceive clearly that which others overlook."[3]

Non-Essentialists listen too. But they listen while preparing to say something. They get distracted by extraneous noise. They hyperfocus on inconsequential details. They hear the loudest voice but they get the wrong message. In their eagerness to react they miss the point. As a result they may, using a metaphor from C. S. Lewis, run around with fire extinguishers in times of flood.[4] They miss the lead.

Non-Essentialist	Essentialist
Pays attention to the loudest voice	Pays attention to the signal in the noise
Hears everything being said	Hears what is *not* being said
Is overwhelmed by all the information	Scans to find the essence of the information

In the chaos of the modern workplace, with so many loud voices all around us pulling us in many directions, it is more important now than ever that we learn to resist the siren song of distraction and keep our eyes and ears peeled for the headlines. Here are a few ways to tap into your inner journalist.

Keep a Journal

Stating the obvious, the words *journal* and *journalist* come from the same root word. A journalist is, in the word's most literal sense, someone who writes a journal. Therefore, one of the most obvious and yet powerful ways to become a journalist of our own lives is simply to keep a journal.

The sad reality is that we humans are forgetful creatures. I would even go so far as to say shockingly forgetful. Don't believe me? You can test this theory right now by trying to recall from memory what you ate for dinner two weeks ago on Thursday. Or ask yourself what meetings you attended three weeks ago on Monday. If you are like most people you will draw a total blank on this exercise. Think of a journal as like a storage device for backing up your brain's faulty hard drive. As someone once said to me, the faintest pencil is better than the strongest memory.

For the last ten years now I have kept a journal, using a counterintuitive yet effective method. It is simply this: I write less than I feel like writing. Typically, when people start to keep a journal they write pages the first day. Then by the second day the prospect of writing so much is daunting, and they procrastinate or abandon the exercise. So apply the principle of "less but better" to your journal. Restrain yourself from writing more until daily journaling has become a habit.

I also suggest that once every ninety days or so you take an hour to read your journal entries from that period. But don't be overly focused on the details, like the budget meeting three weeks ago or last Thursday's pasta dinner. Instead, focus on the broader patterns or trends. Capture the headline. Look for the lead in your day, your week, your life. Small, incremental changes are hard to see in the moment but over time can have a huge cumulative effect.

Get Out into the Field

Jane Chen was one of a team of students in a d.school class called "Design for Extreme Affordability." The class challenged them to design a baby incubator for 1 per cent of the traditional $20,000 cost. According to Jane, in the developing world "4 million low-birthweight children die within the first 28 days because they don't have enough fat to regulate their body temperature."[5]

If they had raced into this as simply a cost problem, they would have produced an inexpensive electric incubator – a seemingly reasonable solution but one that, as it turned out, would have failed to address the root of the problem. Instead, they took the time to find out what really mattered. They went to Nepal to see the challenge firsthand. That's when they discovered 80 per cent of babies were born at home, not in hospital, in rural villages with no electricity. Thus the team's real challenge, it suddenly became clear, was to create something that did not require electricity at all. With that key insight they began in earnest to solve the problem at hand. Eventually Jane and three other teammates launched a non-profit company called "Embrace" and created the "Embrace Nest," which uses a waxlike substance that is heated in water, then placed in the sleeping bag-like pod, where it can warm a baby for six hours or more. By getting out there and fully exploring the problem, they were able to better clarify the question and in turn to focus on the essential details that ultimately allowed them to make the highest contribution to the problem.

Keep your eyes peeled for abnormal or unusual details

Mariam Semaan is an award-winning journalist from Lebanon. She recently completed a John S. Knight Journalism Fellowship at Stanford University, where she specialised in media innovation and design thinking. I asked her to share the secret tips of her trade based on her years of experience capturing the real story amid all of the surface noise. Her reaction was encouraging: she said finding the lead and spotting the essential information are skills that can be acquired. She said, you need knowledge. Getting to the essence of a story takes a deep understanding of the topic, its context, its fit into the bigger picture, and its relationship to different fields. So she would read all the related news and try to spot the one piece of information that all others had missed or hadn't focused enough on. "My goal," she said, "was to understand the 'spiderweb' of the story because that is what allowed me to spot any 'abnormal' or 'unusual' detail or behaviour that didn't quite fit into the natural course of the story."

It's crucial, Mariam says, to seek "a different perspective on a given story, one that would shed the light on the topic in a fresh, different or thought-provoking way." One trick she uses is role play: she puts herself in the shoes of all the main players in a story in order to better understand their motives, reasoning, and points of view.

Clarify the Question

Anyone who has watched skilled politicians being interviewed knows how well trained they can be in not answering the question being asked. Evading hard questions can be tempting for us all. Often it's easier to give a vague, blanket answer rather than to summon up the facts and information required to give a thoughtful, informed answer. Yet evasiveness only sends us down a non-essential spiral of further vagueness and misinformation. Clarifying the question is a way out of that cycle.

Elay Cohen, senior vice president at Salesforce.com, was one member of a six-person team crammed into a hot hotel room at the normally tranquil Cavallo Point, overlooking the Golden Gate Bridge in San Francisco. For the next three hours they would compete against five other teams in a business simulation. The task involved answering a series of questions about how they would handle hypothetical management situations. As the timer ticked, Elay's team was having trouble getting started. Each proposed answer spawned still more opinions and comments, and soon what should have been a fairly straightforward problem-solving exercise had devolved into a sprawling, undisciplined debate. I was there to observe and coach the team, and after fifteen minutes of this I had to ask the team to stop. "What question are you trying to answer?" I asked them. Everyone paused awkwardly. Nobody had a response. Then someone made a comment about something else, and again the group went off on a tangent.

I stepped in and posed my question again. And again. Eventually the team stopped and really thought about what goals they were trying to accomplish and what decisions really needed to be made to accomplish them. They stopped the side conversations. They waded through all the ideas and opinions that had been haphazardly thrown out, listening for the hidden themes and big ideas that connected them. Then, finally, they moved from a state of motion sickness to momentum. They settled on a plan of action, made the necessary decisions, and divided up responsibilities. Elay's team won by a landslide.

CHAPTER 7

PLAY

Embrace the Wisdom of Your Inner Child

A LITTLE NONSENSE NOW AND THEN,
IS CHERISHED BY THE WISEST MEN.

– Roald Dahl

At the end of the classic musical *Mary Poppins* the gruff and joyless Mr Banks arrives home, having been "sacked, discharged, flung into the street." Yet he seems absolutely and uncharacteristically delighted – so delighted that one of the servants concludes he's "gone off his crumpet" and even his son observes, "It doesn't sound like Father." Indeed, his father is almost a new person as he presents his children with their mended kite and launches into the song "Let's Go Fly a Kite." Freed from the dreary tedium of his job at the bank, Banks's inner child suddenly comes alive. The effect of his good cheer is magnificent, lifting the spirits of the whole house and infusing the previously melancholic Banks family with joy, camaraderie, and delight. Yes, it is a fictional story, but it illustrates the powerful effects of restoring play to our daily lives.

The majority of us were not formally taught how to play when we were children; we picked it up naturally and instinctively. Picture a newborn baby's pure joy as a mother plays peekaboo.

Think of a group of children unleashing their imaginations playing make-believe games together. Imagine a child in a state of what Mihaly Csikszentmihalyi calls *flow* as he constructs his own mini kingdom out of a bunch of old cardboard boxes.[1] But then as we get older something happens. We are introduced to the idea that play is trivial. Play is a waste of time. Play is unnecessary. Play is childish. Unfortunately, many of these negative messages come from the very place where imaginative play should be most encouraged, not stifled.

The word *school* is derived from the Greek word *schole,* meaning "leisure." Yet our modern school system, born in the Industrial Revolution, has removed the leisure – and much of the pleasure – out of learning. Sir Ken Robinson, who has made the study of creativity in schools his life's work, has observed that instead of fuelling creativity through play, schools can actually kill it: "We have sold ourselves into a fast-food model of education, and it's impoverishing our spirit and our energies as much as fast food is depleting our physical bodies. . . . Imagination is the source of every form of human achievement. And it's the one thing that I believe we are systematically jeopardizing in the way we educate our children and ourselves."[2] In this he is correct.

This idea that play is trivial stays with us as we reach adulthood and only becomes more ingrained as we enter the workplace. Sadly, not only do far too few companies and organisations foster play; many unintentionally undermine it. True, some companies and executives give lip service to the value of play in sparking creativity, yet most still fail to create the kind of playful culture that sparks true exploration.

None of this should surprise us. Modern corporations were born out of the Industrial Revolution, when their entire reason for being was to achieve efficiency in the mass production of goods.

Furthermore, these early managers looked to the military – a rather less-than-playful entity – for their inspiration (indeed, the language of the military is still strong in corporations today; we still often talk of employees being on the *front lines,* and the word *company* itself is a term for a military unit). While the industrial era is long behind us, those mores, structures, and systems continue to pervade most modern organisations.

Play, which I would define as anything we do simply for the joy of doing rather than as a means to an end – whether it's flying a kite or listening to music or kicking around a football – might seem like a non-essential activity. Often it is treated that way. But in fact play *is* essential in many ways. Stuart Brown, the founder of the National Institute for Play, has studied what are called the play histories of some six thousand individuals and has concluded that play has the power to significantly improve everything from personal health to relationships to education to organisations' ability to innovate. "Play," he says, "leads to brain plasticity, adaptability, and creativity." As he succinctly puts it, "Nothing fires up the brain like play."[3]

Non-Essentialist	Essentialist
Thinks play is trivial	Knows play is essential
Thinks play is an unproductive waste of time	Knows play sparks exploration

A Mind Invited to Play

The value of play in our lives can't be overstated. Studies from the animal kingdom reveal that play is so crucial to the development of key cognitive skills it may even play a role in a species' survival. Bob Fagan, a researcher who has spent fifteen years studying the behaviour of grizzly bears, discovered bears that played the most tended to survive the longest. When asked why, he said, "In a world continuously presenting unique challenges and ambiguity, play prepares these bears for a changing planet."[4]

Jaak Panksepp concluded something similar in *Affective Neuroscience: The Foundations of Human and Animal Emotions*, where he wrote, "One thing is certain, during play, animals are especially prone to behave in flexible and creative ways."[5]

Yet of all animal species, Stuart Brown writes, humans are the biggest players of all. We are built to play and built through play. When we play, we are engaged in the purest expression of our humanity, the truest expression of our individuality. Is it any wonder that often the times we feel most alive, those that make up our best memories, are moments of play?

Play expands our minds in ways that allow us to explore: to germinate new ideas or see old ideas in a new light. It makes us more inquisitive, more attuned to novelty, more engaged. Play is fundamental to living the way of the Essentialist because it fuels exploration in at least three specific ways.

First, play broadens the range of options available to us. It helps us to see possibilities we otherwise wouldn't have seen and make connections we would otherwise not have made. It opens our minds and broadens our perspective. It helps us challenge old assumptions and makes us more receptive to untested ideas. It gives us permission to expand our own stream of consciousness and come up with new stories. Or as Albert Einstein once said: "When I examine myself and my methods of thought, I come to the conclusion that the gift of fantasy has meant more to me than my talent for absorbing positive knowledge."[6]

Second, play is an antidote to stress, and this is key because stress, in addition to being an enemy of productivity, can actually shut down the creative, inquisitive, exploratory parts of our brain. You know how it feels: you're stressed about work and suddenly everything starts going wrong. You can't find your keys, you bump into things more easily, you forget the critical report on the kitchen table. Recent findings suggest this is because stress increases the activity in the part of the brain that monitors emotions (the amygdala), while reducing the activity in the part responsible for cognitive function (the hippocampus)[7] – the result being, simply, that we really can't think clearly.

I have seen play reverse these effects in my own children. When they are stressed and things feel out of control, I get them to draw. When they do, the change is almost immediate. The stress melts away and their ability to explore is regained.

Third, as Edward M. Hallowell, a psychiatrist who specialises in brain science, explains, play has a positive effect on the executive function of the brain. "The brain's executive functions," he writes, "include planning, prioritizing, scheduling, anticipating, delegating, deciding, analyzing – in short, most of the skills any executive must master in order to excel in business."[8]

Play stimulates the parts of the brain involved in both careful, logical reasoning *and* carefree, unbound exploration. Given that, it should hardly be surprising that key breakthroughs in thinking have taken place in times of play. Hallowell writes: "Columbus was at play when it dawned on him that the world was round. Newton was at play in his mind when he saw the apple tree and suddenly conceived of the force of gravity. Watson and Crick were playing with possible shapes of the DNA molecule when they stumbled upon the double helix. Shakespeare played with iambic pentameter his whole life. Mozart barely lived a waking moment when he was not at play. Einstein's thought experiments are brilliant examples of the mind invited to play."[9]

Of Work and Play

Some innovative companies are finally waking up to the essential value of play. The CEO of Twitter, Dick Costolo, promotes play through comedy; he instigated an improv class at the company. As a former stand-up comedian, he knows that improv forces people to stretch their minds and think more flexibly, unconventionally, and creatively.

Other companies promote playfulness through their physical environments. IDEO conducts meetings inside a Microbus. In the halls of Google you're likely to stumble upon (in one example of many) a large dinosaur covered in pink flamingos. At Pixar studios, artists' "offices" may be decorated like anything from an old-time western saloon to a wooden hut (the one that most amazed me when I visited was the one lined floor to ceiling with thousands of *Star Wars* figurines).

A successful woman I once knew at a publishing company kept an Easy Button™ from Staples on her desk. Any time anyone left her office, they would enjoy the childish thrill of slamming their palm down on the big red button – causing a recorded voice to loudly announce to the entire office, "That was easy!" And another woman down the corridor at that same company had a framed poster in her office of a children's book illustration to remind her of the joy of childhood reading.

Desk toys, dinosaurs covered with flamingos, and offices full of action figures may seem like trivial diversions to some, but the very point is that they can be the exact opposite. These efforts *challenge* the non-Essentialist logic that play is trivial. Instead, they celebrate play as a vital driver of creativity and exploration.

Play doesn't just help us to explore what is essential. It *is* essential in and of itself.

So how can we all introduce more play into our workplaces and our lives? In his book, Brown includes a primer to help readers reconnect with play. He suggests that readers mine their past for play memories. What did you do as a child that excited you? How can you recreate that today?

Chapter 8

SLEEP

Protect the Asset

Each night, when I go to sleep,
I die. And the next morning,
when I wake up, I am reborn.

– Mahatma Gandhi

Geoff sat straight up in bed, in a panic. He felt as if a bomb had exploded in his head. He was sweating and discombobulated. He listened intensely. What was going on? Everything was silent. Perhaps it was a weird reaction to something he'd eaten. He tried to go back to sleep.

The next night it happened again. Then a few days later it happened in the middle of the day. He had just returned from India and at first he thought it might be a reaction to malaria medicine he was taking in combination with the Benadryl he took to help him sleep when he was jet-lagged. But as his situation worsened he found his condition was more complicated. It was like he was experiencing anxiety attacks but without any anxiety – just the physical symptoms.

Geoff was a textbook overachiever who had a deep desire to make a difference (to give some context for this, his grandfather was an early administrator in the US Peace Corps). Geoff was fiercely ambitious, driven, and committed to making a contribution to the world: he was on the board of Kiva Microfunds, he had been named Ernst and Young's Entrepreneur of the Year and a Young Global Leader by the World Economic Forum, he was the co-founder of a successful impact investment fund, and he was the CEO of a global microcredit organization that was reaching more than 12 million poor families around the world. He was thirty-six years old and on top of his game.

Geoff travelled constantly, which often made sleep difficult. His company was based in Seattle but had offices in San Francisco, India, and Kenya. He would routinely fly to London for meetings, then to India for six days to be in five different cities, to Geneva for hours of meetings with investors, and then back to Seattle for a day and a half. For three years he travelled 60 to 70 per cent of the time. On average, he slept about four to six hours a night.

But at the ripe age of thirty-six, his pace of work was starting to threaten his health and his ability to contribute. What started with the nighttime attacks worsened. One by one each of his organs started shutting down. His heart rate was erratic. It became painful to stand up straight. He had to blend his food because he could not digest it. His blood pressure was so low he blacked out if he stood up too fast. He ended up in casuality twice. He kept telling himself he would slow down after the next deal, then the next, then the one after that. But of course he didn't. He was sure that if he just kept going he could work his way out of this. He didn't want to face the trade-offs that scaling back entailed. But they soon caught up with him: he would be forced to cancel meetings at the last minute because he was too weak to attend or he would give a speech but bomb it because his brain was cloudy. He started to wonder if he was doing the company more harm than good – and he definitely was.

Eventually, after a clear diagnosis, he was given two options by his doctor: he could take medication for the rest of his life to deal with his symptoms, or he could disengage from everything for a year or two to treat and recover from his illness. Geoff didn't accept this trade-off at first. He was a competitive triathlete, and he thought he could apply the same logic he would to an ankle sprain or a torn rotator cuff. He boastfully told the doctor he would take a couple of months off and be back to full form: "Watch! Just watch!"

He took a two-month sabbatical, and to his surprise he totally crashed. He slept fourteen hours per night! Then he rested all day long. He could not even get out of bed some days. He was totally nonfunctional for six weeks. He came crawling back in to his doctor and admitted this was going to take a lot longer than a couple of months.

True to his word, he got rid of everything that was creating stress in his life. He resigned from his boards and decided to leave his company too. He said: "The decision to disengage was very, very difficult. I walked out of the board meeting, tears in my eyes, and said to my wife, 'This is not how I wanted to leave my baby!'"

He designed a life totally devoted to regeneration and recuperation as he went through the treatment protocol. He changed his diet. He went to the South of France for a year with his family. The treatment and change in climate and lifestyle worked. With a new mind-set, he began to think about what he had learned through the experience.

Two and a half years later, Geoff was in Tanzania for a Young Global Leaders event with the World Economic Forum. One evening at an open-mic night Geoff was urged by those who knew his story to share what he had learned with the group of two hundred accomplished peers. Through great emotion, he told them that he had paid a high price to learn a simple yet essential lesson: "Protect the asset."

Protecting the Asset

The best asset we have for making a contribution to the world is *ourselves*. If we underinvest in ourselves, and by that I mean our minds, our bodies, and our spirits, we damage the very tool we need to make our highest contribution. One of the most common ways people – especially ambitious, successful people – damage this asset is through a lack of sleep.

If we let our type A instincts take over, we will, like Geoff, be swallowed up whole. We will burn out too early. We need to be as strategic with ourselves as we are with our careers and our businesses. We need to pace ourselves, nurture ourselves, and give ourselves fuel to explore, thrive, and perform.

In the many hours Geoff spent resting he came to see an interesting paradox in his addiction to achievement: for a type A personality, it is *not* hard to push oneself hard. Pushing oneself to the limit is easy! The real challenge for the person who thrives on challenges is *not* to work hard. He explains to any overachievers: "If you think you are so tough you can do anything I have a challenge for you. If you really want to do something hard: say no to an opportunity so you can take a nap."

By the time I was twenty-one I too thought of sleep as something to be avoided. To me, it was a necessary evil: a waste of time that could otherwise be spent productively, something for the weak, or the weak-willed. The vision of being superhuman and sleeping only a few hours a night was intoxicating. I even experimented with some rather drastic and unconventional ways to try to cut down on sleep. After reading a sleep study where some participants were required to sleep only twenty minutes every four hours around the clock, I tried it out. It was bearable for a while, but I soon found that while you can technically survive on this schedule of sleep it has its drawbacks. For example, while I was technically awake, my brain was just barely functioning. It was harder to think, plan, prioritise, or see the bigger picture. It was hard to make decisions or choices and nearly impossible to discern the essential from the trivial.

It soon became unsustainable, but still I was determined that the less I slept, the more I could get done. So I adopted the new tactic of pulling one all-nighter per week. This was not much better. Then my wife, who did not care for this practice, gave me an article that completely shifted the way I saw sleep. It challenged the notion that sleep was an enemy of productivity, convincingly arguing that in fact sleep was a driver of peak performance. I remember the article cited top business leaders who boasted about getting a full eight hours. I also remember Bill Clinton was quoted as saying that every major mistake he had made in his life had happened as a result of sleep deprivation. Ever since, I have tried to get eight hours a night.

What about you? Think about the last week. Have you slept less than seven hours on any of those nights? Have you slept less than seven hours for a few nights in a row? Have you caught yourself saying or thinking proudly: *"Not me. I don't need the full eight hours. I can totally survive on four or five hours of sleep"* (if you thought that right now while reading this, you will get a lot out of this chapter). Well, while there are clearly people who can survive on fewer hours of sleep, I've found that most of them are just so used to being tired they have forgotten what it really feels like to be fully rested.

The way of the non-Essentialist is to see sleep as yet another burden on one's already overextended, overcommitted, busy-but-not-always-productive life. Essentialists instead see sleep as necessary for operating at high levels of contribution more of the time. This is why they systematically and deliberately build sleep into their schedules so they can do more, achieve more, and explore more. By "protecting their asset" they are able to go about their daily lives with a reserve of energy, creativity, and problem-solving ability to call upon when needed – unlike non-Essentialists, who can never know when and where they'll be hijacked by their own fatigue.

Essentialists choose to do one fewer thing right now in order to do more tomorrow. Yes, it is a trade-off. But cumulatively, this small trade-off can yield big rewards.

Non-Essentialist	Essentialist
THINKS:	**KNOWS:**
One hour less of sleep equals one more hour of productivity.	One hour more of sleep equals several more hours of much higher productivity.
Sleep is for failures.	Sleep is for high performers.
Sleep is a luxury.	Sleep is a priority.
Sleep breeds laziness.	Sleep breeds creativity.
Sleep gets in the way of "doing it all."	Sleep enables the highest levels of mental contribution.

Shattering the Sleep Stigma

So if "protecting the asset" is so important, why do we give up our precious sleep so easily? For overachievers part of the reason may be that they simply subscribe to the false belief, as I did, that if they sleep less they will achieve more. Yet there are ample reasons to challenge this assumption, like the growing body of research demonstrating that a good night's sleep actually makes us *more* productive, not less.

In K. Anders Ericsson's famous study of violinists, popularised by Malcolm Gladwell as "the 10,000-Hour Rule," Anders found that the best violinists spent more time practising than the merely good students.[1] His finding supports Essentialist logic by showing that mastery takes focused and deliberate effort, and indeed it's encouraging to learn that excellence is within our sphere of influence rather than a blessing bestowed only on the most naturally gifted. But it also comes dangerously close to encouraging the non-Essentialist mind-set of "I have to do it all," the pernicious myth that can lead people to justify spending longer and longer hours working, with diminishing returns.

That is, until we look at a less well-known finding from the same study: that the *second* most important factor differentiating the best violinists from the good violinists was actually *sleep*. The best violinists slept an average of 8.6 hours in every twenty-four-hour period: about an hour longer than average. Over the period of a week they also spent an average of 2.8 hours napping in the afternoon: about two hours longer than the average. Sleep, the authors of the study concluded, allowed these top performers to regenerate so that they could practise with greater concentration. So yes, while they practised more, they *also got more out of those hours of practise* because they were better rested.

In a *Harvard Business Review* article called "Sleep Deficit: The Performance Killer," Charles A. Czeisler, the Baldino Professor of Sleep Medicine at Harvard Medical School, has explained how sleep deprivation undermines high performance. He likens sleep deficit to drinking too much alcohol, explaining that pulling an all-nighter (i.e. going twenty-four hours without sleep) or having a week of sleeping just four or five hours a night actually "induces an impairment equivalent to a blood alcohol level of 0.1%. Think about this: we would never say, 'This person is a great worker! He's drunk all the time!' yet we continue to celebrate people who sacrifice sleep for work."[2]

While sleep is often associated with giving rest to the body, recent research shows that sleep is really more about the brain. Indeed, a study from Lüebeck University in Germany provides evidence that a full night's sleep may actually increase brain power and enhance our problem-solving ability.

In the study, reported by the journal *Nature,* over one hundred volunteers were given a number puzzle with an unconventional twist; it required finding a "hidden code" to uncover the answer.[3] The volunteers were divided into two groups; one was allowed an eight-hour stretch of uninterrupted sleep and another group received interrupted sleep. The scientists then watched to see which volunteers found the hidden code and how quickly they found it. The result was that *twice* the number of people who had slept for eight hours solved the problem than the volunteers from the sleep-deprived group. Why? The researchers explained that while we sleep our brains are hard at work encoding and restructuring information. Therefore, when we wake up, our brains may have made new neural connections, thereby opening up a broader range of solutions to problems, literally overnight.

Some good news for the early birds and night owls among us: science shows that even a nap can increase creativity. In just one example, a report from the *Proceedings of the National Academy of Sciences* revealed that even a single REM – or rapid eye movement – cycle enhanced the integration of unassociated information. Even a brief period of deep sleep, in other words, helps us make the kinds of new connections that allow us to better explore our world.

In a nutshell, sleep is what allows us to operate at our highest level of contribution so that we can achieve more, in less time.

While there continues to be a culture of machismo when it comes to going without sleep, luckily the stigma is fading, thanks in part to a few super-high performers – particularly in industries that typically celebrate burning the candle at both ends – who have publicly boasted about getting a full eight hours. These people – many of them true Essentialists – know their healthy sleep habits give them a huge competitive advantage, and they are right.

Jeff Bezos, the founder of Amazon.com, is one of them. He says: "I'm more alert and I think more clearly. I just feel so much better all day long if I've had eight hours." Mark Andreessen, co-founder of Netscape, and a reformed sleep restrictor who used to work till the early hours but still be up at 7 a.m., is another. He said, "I would spend the whole day wishing I could go home and go back to bed." Now he says of his level of sleep: "Seven [hours] and I start to degrade. Six is suboptimal. Five is a big problem. Four means I'm a zombie." At weekends he sleeps twelve-plus hours. "It makes a big difference in my ability to function," he said.

These executives are quoted in an article called "Sleep Is the New Status Symbol for Successful Entrepreneurs."[4] Nancy Jeffrey of the *Wall Street Journal* writes: "It's official. Sleep, that rare commodity in stressed-out America, is the new status symbol. Once derided as a wimpish failing – the same 1980s overachievers who cried 'Lunch is for Losers' also believed 'Sleep is for Suckers' – slumber is now being touted as the restorative companion to the creative executive mind." To this we can add that it is also the restorative companion to the discerning Essentialist mind.

In another article in the *New York Times*, Erin Callan, the former chief financial officer of Lehman Brothers, tells the story of how "at an office party in 2005, one of my colleagues asked my then husband what I did on weekends. She knew me as someone with great intensity and energy. 'Does she kayak, go rock climbing and then run a half marathon?' she joked. No, he answered simply, 'she sleeps.' And that was true. When I wasn't catching up on work, I spent my weekends recharging my batteries for the coming week."[5]

So if the stigma of sleep still exists in your workplace, consider developing an initiative at work to explicitly encourage sleep. If that sounds radical, consider how the many benefits of sleep – greater creativity, enhanced productivity, even lower health care costs – have the potential to directly affect the bottom line. With this perspective, it is not so hard to imagine encouraging your manager or HR department to develop a written policy (after all, many companies have policies addressing alcohol consumption, and, as we have seen, the parallels in how alcohol and sleep deprivation affect performance are real). For example, Charles Czeisler at Harvard has proposed a policy that no employee is expected to drive into work after a red-eye flight, and other companies allow employees to come in late after staying late at work the previous night. Companies and leaders like these know that "protecting their assets" is a matter of fiduciary responsibility.

Under the auspices of book research, I recently went to Google to take a nap in one of their famous nap pods. It was a white spaceship pod (like something you might imagine seeing on the seventies TV show *Mork and Mindy*), of about twenty square feet, big enough to lie down but not completely flat. It had a dome-shaped cover that concealed most but not all of my body, and as a result I was a little self-conscious at first and wondered whether I would be able to fall asleep. Thirty minutes later, as the pod vibrated gently to let me know my session was over, I didn't have to wonder.

When I woke up from the nap I could really feel how much I had needed it. I felt clearer, sharper, more alert.

To use the pods at Google there is a calendar sign-up. How many people used it the week I was there? I wondered. Of the fifty people who work on the floor where it is situated, I imagined at least ten or twenty. Wrong. According to the calendar, just a single person had taken this opportunity to recharge brain and body with thirty minutes of midday sleep. Nevertheless, even the presence of the pod is important in signalling to employees that sleep is a priority.

Our highest priority is to protect our ability to prioritise.

In this section of the book we have been talking about how to explore and evaluate options in order to discern the essential few from the many trivial, mediocre, or even just good. By definition this is a process of prioritisation. It includes the challenge of filtering options that, at first glance, *all* look important. Yet as the logic of an Essentialist explains, in reality there are only a few things of exceptional value, with almost everything else being of far less importance. The problem with being sleep-deprived is that it compromises our ability to tell the difference, and thus our precious ability to prioritise.

Sleep will enhance your ability to explore, make connections, and do less but better throughout your waking hours.

CHAPTER 9

SELECT

The Power of Extreme Criteria

AN INNER PROCESS STANDS IN NEED
OF OUTWARD CRITERIA.

—*Ludwig Wittgenstein*

In a piece called "No More Yes. It's Either HELL YEAH! Or No," the popular TED speaker Derek Sivers describes a simple technique for becoming more selective in the choices we make. The key is to put the decision to an extreme test: if we feel total and utter conviction to do something, then we say yes, Derek-style. *Anything* less gets a thumbs down. Or as a leader at Twitter once put it to me, "*If the answer isn't a definite yes then it should be a no.*" It is a succinct summary of a core Essentialist principle, and one that is critical to the process of exploration.[1]

Derek lives this principle himself. When he wasn't blown away by any of the candidates he interviewed for a job, he said no to all of them. Eventually he found exactly the right person. When he realised he had signed up for several conferences around the world that he wasn't really enthusiastic about, he decided to stay home and skip all of them, and in turn earned twelve days he used to more productive ends. When he was trying to decide where to live, he ruled out places that seemed pretty good (Sydney and Vancouver) until he visited New York and knew instantly it was exactly the right place for him.

Think back to what happens to our wardrobes when we use the broad criterion, "Is there a chance that I will wear this someday in the future?" The wardrobe becomes cluttered with clothes we rarely wear. But if we ask, "Do I absolutely *love* this?" then we will be able to eliminate the clutter and have space for something better. We can do the same with other choices – whether big or small, significant or trivial – in every area of our lives.

The 90 Per Cent Rule

Recently, a colleague and I were working to select twenty-four people from a pool of almost one hundred applicants to our "Design Your Life, Essentially" class. First, we identified a set of minimum criteria such as "Can attend every class." Then we settled on a set of ideal attributes like "Is ready for a life-changing experience." Using these criteria, we scored each candidate on a 1 to 10 scale. The 9s and 10s, we decided, were obviously in. Anyone under a 7 was automatically out. I was then given the unenviable task of evaluating the in-between candidates: the 7s and 8s. As I struggled to determine which of these candidates would be good enough, I had the thought: if something (or in this case someone) is *just* or *almost* good enough – that is, a 7 or an 8 – then the answer should be a *no*. It was so liberating.

You can think of this as the 90 Per Cent Rule, and it's one you can apply to just about every decision or dilemma. As you evaluate an option, think about the single most important criterion for that decision, and then simply give the option a score between 0 and 100. If you rate it any lower than 90 per cent, then automatically change the rating to 0 and simply reject it. This way you avoid getting caught up in indecision, or worse, getting stuck with the 60s or 70s. Think about how you'd feel if you scored a 65 on some test. Why would you deliberately choose to feel that way about an important choice in your life?

Mastering this Essentialist skill, perhaps more than any other in this section, requires us to be vigilant about acknowledging the reality of trade-offs. By definition, applying highly selective criteria is a trade-off; sometimes you will have to turn down a seemingly very good option and have faith that the perfect option will soon come along. Sometimes it will, and sometimes it won't, but the point is that the very act of applying selective criteria forces *you* to choose which perfect option to wait for, rather than letting other people, or the universe, choose for you. Like any Essentialist skill, it forces you to make decisions by design, rather than default.

The benefits of this ultra-selective approach to decision making in all areas of our lives should be clear: when our selection criteria are too broad, we will find ourselves committing to too many options. What's more, assigning simple numerical values to our options forces us to make decisions consciously, logically, and rationally, rather than impulsively or emotionally. Yes, it takes discipline to apply tough criteria. But failing to do so carries a high cost.

Non-Essentialists apply implicit or unspoken criteria to the decisions they make in both their personal and their professional lives. For example, when deciding what projects to take on at work, a non-Essentialist may operate by the implicit criterion, "If my manager asks me to do it, then I should do it." Or even more broadly, "If someone asks me to do something, I should try to do it." Or still more broadly, "If other people in the company are doing it, I should be doing it." In an era of social media where we are vastly more aware of what other people are doing, this criterion can create a particularly serious burden by amplifying all of the non-essential activities we "should" be doing.

Non-Essentialist	Essentialist
Says yes to almost every request or opportunity	Says yes to only the top 10 per cent of opportunities
Uses broad, implicit criteria like "If someone I know is doing it, I should do it."	Uses narrow, explicit criteria like "Is this *exactly* what I am looking for?"

One executive team I worked with had at one time identified three criteria for deciding what projects to take on. But over time they had become more and more indiscriminate, and eventually the company's portfolio of projects seemed to share only the criterion that a customer had asked them to do it. As a result, the morale on the team had plummeted, and not simply because team members were overworked and overwhelmed from having taken on too much. It was also because no project ever seemed to justify itself, and there was no greater sense of purpose. Worse, it now became difficult to distinguish themselves in the marketplace because their work, which had previously occupied a unique and profitable niche, had become so general.

Only by going through the work of identifying extreme criteria were they able to get rid of the 70 and 80 per cents that were draining their time and resources and start focusing on the most interesting work that best distinguished them in the marketplace. Furthermore, this system empowered employees to choose the projects on which they could make their highest contribution; where they had once been at the mercy of what felt like capricious management decisions, they now had a voice. On one occasion I saw the quietest and most junior member of the team push back on the most senior executive. She simply said, "Should we be taking on this account, given the criteria we have?" This had never happened until the criteria were made both selective and explicit.

Making our criteria both selective and explicit affords us a systematic tool for discerning what is essential and filtering out the things that are not.

Selective, Explicit, and Also Right

Mark Adams, the managing director of Vitsoe, has spent the last twenty-seven years deliberately applying selective criteria to his work.

Vitsoe makes furniture. The furniture industry is notorious for churning out a high volume of product: each season brings a vast offering of new colours and styles. Yet Vitsoe has for decades offered only one product: the 606 Universal Shelving System. Why? Because quite simply, Vitsoe has very particular standards, and the 606 Universal Shelving system is the only product that makes the cut.

The 606 System epitomises the Essentialist ethic of "less but better" discussed in chapter 1 and advocated by Dieter Rams. This is more than coincidence, given that the 606 Universal Shelving System was designed by Dieter. But Vitsoe's approach to hiring may be more selective still.

They begin with the basic assumption that they would rather be understaffed than hire the wrong person quickly. Accordingly, when they are looking for a new employee, they have a rigorous and systematic selection process. First, they interview someone by phone. This is deliberate because they want to strip away all visual cues while forming their first impression. Equally, they want to hear how the prospective employee performs on the phone and whether the employee is organised enough to find a quiet place at an allotted time. They weed out many at this stage – in a time-efficient manner.

Second, a candidate is interviewed by multiple people throughout the company. If a candidate makes it through several interviews, he or she is invited to spend a day working with the team. Then management sends a questionnaire out to the whole team asking them how they feel about the candidate. But instead of just the obvious questions, they ask, "Would he or she *love* working here?" and "Would we *love* having him or her work with us?" No offer is made at this point, and no commitment is implied on the part of the candidate. The objective is to allow both sides to see each other as honestly as possible. If the fit is just right, the candidate will continue through the final interviews and may receive an offer. If the team isn't absolutely sure, then the answer is *no*.

Once they had a candidate applying for a job on the shelving installation team. It is an important role; these installers are the face of the product and the company. The candidate in question did a good job installing the shelving system. But in the debrief with Mark afterwards the team had a concern. At the end of the day, when they were packing up their tools, the candidate just threw the tools into the box and closed the lid. To you and me, this would seem a minor infraction – hardly significant enough to mention, let alone overshadow a day's worth of otherwise flawless work. But to the team it signified a carelessness that didn't jibe with their vision of the ideal person for the job. Mark listened and agreed, then politely told the candidate he wasn't the right fit with the Vitsoe culture. For Mark and his team:

If it isn't a clear *yes*, then it's a clear *no*.

But undergirding their highly selective screening process is more than a gut reaction (although that matters too). What may seem like a capricious decision is really the result of a disciplined and continuous approach to figure out what works and what doesn't. For example, they have learned there is a high correlation between how intensely someone played with Lego as a child and how well he or she will fit with the Vitsoe culture. They didn't pick that out of the air. They have tried all manner of things over the years; some have stuck, but many have not.

The team also uses an explicit set of criteria in making their evaluation. Their primary criterion is, "Will this person be an absolutely *natural* fit?" That is why they have designed the selection process to include multiple interviews. That is why they developed the workday trial run. It's why they send the questionnaire. Like any true Essentialist, they are trying to gather the *relevant* information so they can make an informed, calculated, deliberate decision.

Box CEO Aaron Levie has a similar criterion for hiring. He simply asks if the person is someone he'd want to work with every day. "One of the ways we think about this is," he says, "could this person have been one of the founding members of the team?" If the answer is yes, he knows he's found someone who will fit right in.[2]

Opportunity Knocks

Being selective when deciding what opportunities to go after is one thing, but it can get even harder when opportunities come to us. We get a job offer we didn't expect. A side project comes along that isn't really what we do, but it is easy cash. Someone asks us to help out with something we love doing, but it is unpaid work. An acquaintance has a time share available in a less-than-ideal location but at a discounted rate. What do we do?

The fear of missing out goes into full effect. How can we say no; the offer is right here for the taking. We might never have gone after it, but now it is so easy to get it we consider it. But if we just say yes because it is an easy reward, we run the risk of having later to say no to a more meaningful one.

This was the situation Nancy Duarte found herself in when building a communication agency. In 2000, the company was a generalist agency doing everything from creating corporate identities to print and website development to designing presentations (work most designer firms loathed doing). But without one specialty to differentiate them, the company started to become pretty much like any other design agency out there.

Then Nancy read Jim Collins's *Good to Great,* in which he contends if there's one thing you are passionate about – and that you can be best at – you should do *just that one thing.* That's when she realised the real opportunity to differentiate the company might be in the very type of work nobody else in the industry wanted to do: designing presentations.

By focusing on work no one else was doing, they could create the knowledge, tools, and expertise to become the premier company in the world at presentations. But to achieve this they would have to say no to everything else. Even in bad economic times. Even when paid work was offered to them. It was the price for becoming distinct. In other words, they would have to be more selective in the work they took on, so they could channel all their energies towards excelling in the area that had become their speciality.

Here's a simple, systematic process you can use to apply selective criteria to opportunities that come your way. First, write down the opportunity. Second, write down a list of three "minimum criteria" the options would need to "pass" in order to be considered. Third, write down a list of three ideal or "extreme criteria" the options would need to "pass" in order to be considered. By definition, if the opportunity doesn't pass the first set of criteria, the answer is obviously no. But if it also doesn't pass *two of your three* extreme criteria, the answer is still no.

opportunity What opportunity is being offered to you?			
minimum What are your minimum criteria for this option to be considered?			
extreme What are the ideal criteria for this option to be approved?			

The Best Slice of Pizza in Brooklyn

Applying tougher criteria to life's big decisions allows us better to tap into our brain's sophisticated search engine. Think of it as the difference between conducting a Google search for "good restaurant in New York City" and "best slice of pizza in downtown Brooklyn." If we search for "a good career opportunity," our brain will serve up scores of pages to explore and work through. Instead, why not conduct an advanced search and ask three questions: "What am I deeply passionate about?" and "What taps my talent?" and "What meets a significant need in the world?" Naturally there won't be as many pages to view, but that is the point of the exercise. We aren't looking for a plethora of good things to do. We are looking for the *one* where we can make our absolutely highest point of contribution.

Enric Sala is someone who found his life's calling in this way.[3] Early on in his career, Enric was a professor at the prestigious Scripps Institution of Oceanography in La Jolla, California. But he couldn't kick the feeling that the career path he was on was just a close second to the path he should really be on. So he left academia and went to work with *National Geographic*. With that success came new and intriguing opportunities in Washington, D.C., that again left him feeling he was *close* to the right career path but not quite on it yet. As often happens to driven, ambitious people, his earlier success had distracted him from his clarity of purpose. Since the moment he had watched Jacques Cousteau aboard the famed *Calypso* he had dreamed of diving in the world's most beautiful oceans. So after a couple of years, when a golden opportunity presented itself, he changed gears again in order to be where he could truly make his highest contribution: as an explorer-in-residence with *National Geographic*, where he could spend a significant portion of his time diving in the most remote locations while also using his strengths in science and communications to influence policy on a global scale. The price of his dream job was saying no to the many good, even very good, parallel opportunities he encountered and waiting for the one he could enthusiastically say yes to. And the wait was worth it.

Enric is one of those relatively rare examples of someone who is doing work that he loves, that taps his talent, and that serves an important need in the world. His main objective is to help create the equivalent of national parks to protect the last pristine places in the ocean – a truly essential contribution.

eliminate

HOW CAN WE CUT OUT
THE TRIVIAL MANY?

ELIMINATE

How Can We Cut Out the Trivial Many?

Think back to the wardrobe metaphor we talked about in chapter 1. At this point in the book, you've taken stock of everything hanging in your wardrobe. You have your clothes divided into piles of "must keep" and "probably should get rid of." But are you really ready to stuff the "probably should get rid of" pile in a bag and send it off?

In other words, it's not enough to simply determine which activities and efforts don't make the best possible contribution; you still have to actively eliminate those that do not. Part Three of this book will show you how to eliminate the non-essentials so you can make a higher level of contribution towards the things that are actually vital. And not only that, but you'll learn to do it in a way that actually garners you *more* respect from colleagues, bosses, clients, and peers.

Getting rid of those old clothes isn't easy. After all, there is still that nagging reluctance, that nagging fear that "what if" years down the road you come to regret giving away that blazer with the big shoulder pads and loud pinstripes. This feeling is normal; studies have found that we tend to value things we already own more highly than they are worth, and thus find them more difficult to get rid of. If you're not quite ready to part with that metaphorical blazer, ask the killer question: "If I didn't already own this, how much would I spend to buy it?" Likewise, in your life, the killer question when deciding what activities to eliminate is: "If I didn't have this opportunity, what would I be willing to do to acquire it?"

Of course, finding the discipline to say *no* to opportunities – often very good opportunities – that come your way in work and life is infinitely harder than throwing out old clothes from your wardrobe. But find it you must, because remember that anytime you fail to say "no" to a non-essential, you are really saying yes by default. So once you have sufficiently explored your options, the question you should be asking yourself is not: "What, of my list of competing priorities, should I say yes to?" Instead, ask the essential question: "What will I say *no* to?" This is the question that will uncover your true priorities. It is the question that will reveal the best path forward for your team. It is the question that will uncover your true purpose and help you make the highest level of contribution not only to your own goals but to the mission of your organisation. It is that question that can deliver the rare and precious clarity necessary to achieve game-changing breakthroughs in your career, and in your life.

CHAPTER 10

CLARIFY

One Decision That Makes a Thousand

TO FOLLOW, WITHOUT HALT, ONE AIM:
THERE IS THE SECRET TO SUCCESS.

—*Anna Pavlova, Russian ballet dancer*

Let's start with a game. On the next page are mission statements from three companies. Try to match each company with its mission statement:[1]

COMPANY	MISSION STATEMENT

1 AGCO
A chief manufacturer and distributor of agricultural equipment such as replacement parts, tractors, hay tools, and implements.

A "Profitable growth through superior customer service, innovation, quality, and commitment."

2 DOVER CORPORATION
A manufacturer of equipment such as garbage trucks and electronic equipment such as ink-jet printers and circuit board assemblies.

B "To be the leader in every market we serve to the benefit of our customers and our shareholders."

3 DEAN FOODS CORPORATION
A food and beverage company, in particular a milk, dairy, and soy products manufacturer.

C "The Company's primary objective is to maximise long-term stockholder value, while adhering to the laws of the jurisdictions in which it operates and at all times observing the highest ethical standards."

How did you do? If you had absolutely no idea how to solve this puzzle, you are not alone. The largely indistinguishable statements make the task almost impossible. Such vague, inflated mission statements may still be considered "best practice" in some quarters, but in many cases they do not achieve what they were intended to achieve: to inspire their employees with a clear sense of purpose.

This section of the book is all about how to eliminate non-essentials in order to ensure that we can pour our energies into the activities that are most meaningful to us. The first type of non-essential you're going to learn how to eliminate is simply any activity that is misaligned with what you are intending to achieve. It sounds straightforward enough, but to be able to do that you

Answer Code: 1(A), 2(B), and 3(C)

need to be really clear about what your purpose is in the first place – which is where this chapter comes in.

From "Pretty Clear" to "Really Clear"

Executives I work with often suggest their company purpose or strategy is "pretty clear," as if to say that is sufficient. But anyone who wears glasses knows there is a big difference between pretty clear and really clear! The same seems true with individuals' professional strategy. When I ask people, "What do you *really* want out of your career over the next five years?" I am still taken aback by how few people can answer the question.

This would matter less if it were not for the fact that clarity of purpose so consistently predicts how people do their jobs. In working with executive teams I have been amazed to see what happens when teams are only "sort of clear" about what they are trying to achieve rather than "really clear."

For one, there is a heavy price just in terms of human dynamics. The fact is, motivation and cooperation deteriorate when there is a lack of purpose. You can train leaders in communication and teamwork and conduct 360 feedback reports until you are blue in the face, but if a team does not have clarity of goals and roles, problems will fester and multiply.

This is not just my theory or something I read in another business book. In gathering data from more than five hundred people about their experience in more than one thousand teams, I have found a consistent reality: When there is a serious lack of clarity about what the team stands for and what their goals and roles are, people experience confusion, stress, and frustration. When there is a high level of clarity, on the other hand, people thrive.

When there is a lack of clarity, people waste time and energy on the trivial many. When they have sufficient levels of clarity, they are capable of greater breakthroughs and innovations – greater than people even realise they ought to have – in those areas that are truly vital. In my work, I have noticed two common patterns that typically emerge when teams lack clarity of purpose.

PATTERN 1: PLAYING POLITICS

In the first pattern, the team becomes overly focused on winning the attention of the manager. The problem is, when people don't know what the end game is, they are unclear about how to win, and as a result they make up their own game and their own rules as they vie for the manager's favour. Instead of focusing their time and energies on making a high level of contribution, they put all their effort into games like attempting to look better than their peers, demonstrating their self-importance, and echoing their manager's every idea or sentiment. These kinds of activities are not only non-essential but damaging and counterproductive.

We do a similar thing in our personal lives as well. When we are unclear about our real purpose in life – in other words, when we don't have a clear sense of our goals, our aspirations, and our values – we make up our own social games. We waste time and energies on trying to look good in comparison to other people. We overvalue non-essentials like

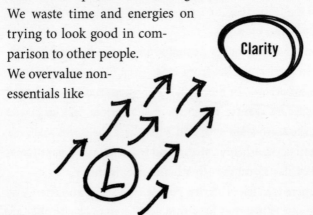

a nicer car or house, or even intangibles like the number of our followers on Twitter or the way we look in our Facebook photos. As a result, we neglect activities that *are* truly essential, like spending time with our loved ones, or nurturing our spirit, or taking care of our health.

PATTERN 2: IT'S ALL GOOD (WHICH IS BAD)

In the second pattern, teams without purpose become leaderless. With no clear direction, people pursue the things that advance their own short-term interests, with little awareness of how their activities contribute to (or in some cases, derail) the long-term mission of the team as a whole. Often these activities are well-intentioned, and some may even be essential on a personal level. But when people are working in teams, many disparate projects that are at odds with each other do not add up to the team's highest level of contribution. Teams like this seem to take five steps back for each step forward.

In the same way, when individuals are involved in too many disparate activities – even good activities – they can fail to achieve their essential mission. One reason for this is that the activities don't work in concert, so they don't add up into a meaningful whole. For example, pursuing five different major subjects, each of them perfectly good, does not equal a degree. Likewise, five different jobs in five different industries do not add up to a forward-moving career. Without clarity and purpose, pursuing something because it is good is not good enough to make a high level of contribution. As Ralph Waldo Emerson said, "The crime which bankrupts men and states is that of job-work; – declining from your main design to serve a turn here or there."

When teams are really clear about their purpose and their individual roles, on the other hand, it is amazing what happens to team dynamics. Formal momentum accelerates, adding up to a higher cumulative contribution of the team as a whole.

So how do we achieve clarity of purpose in our teams and even our personal endeavours? One way is to decide on an essential intent.

Essential Intent

To understand what an essential intent *is,* we may be best served by first establishing what it *is not.*[2] At the risk of using a consulting cliché, we can explore this using a two-by-two matrix.

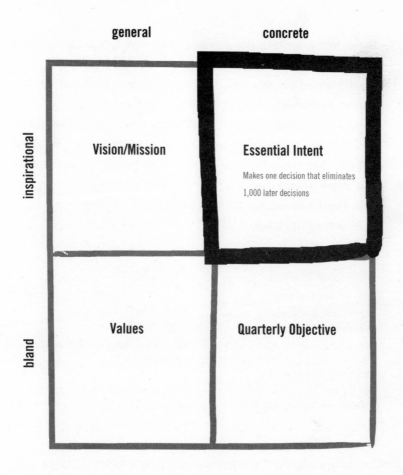

In the top left quadrant, we have vision and mission statements like "We want to change the world": statements that *sound* inspirational but are so general they are almost entirely ignored. In the bottom left quadrant, we have a set of vague, general values – like "innovation," "leadership," and "teamwork" – but these are typically too bland and generic to inspire any passion. In the bottom right quadrant, we have shorter-term quarterly objectives we pay attention to, like "Increase profits 5 per cent over last year's results";

these shorter-term tactics may be concrete enough to get our attention, but they often lack inspiration.

An essential intent, on the other hand, is both inspirational and concrete, both meaningful and measurable. Done right, an essential intent is one decision that settles one thousand later decisions. It's like deciding you're going to become a doctor instead of a lawyer. One strategic choice eliminates a universe of other options and maps a course for the next five, ten, or even twenty years of your life. Once the big decision is made, all subsequent decisions come into better focus.

Non-Essentialist	Essentialist
Has a vague, general vision or mission statement	Has a strategy that is concrete *and* inspirational
Has concrete quarterly objectives but ones that fail to energise or inspire people to take their efforts to the next level	Has an intent that is both meaningful and memorable
Has a value set but no guiding principles for implementing them	Makes one decision that eliminates one thousand later decisions

When Martha Lane Fox was asked by the British prime minister to be the United Kingdom's first "Digital Champion," she had the opportunity to create a description for this newly created role. You can just imagine all the vague, uninspired, or jargony ways Martha might have tried to explain it; it was a *Dilbert* comic strip waiting to happen.

Instead, Martha and her team came up with this essential intent: "To get everyone in the UK online by the end of 2012." It was simple, concrete, inspiring, and easily measured. It gave everyone in the team clarity about exactly what they were trying to do, so they could coordinate their actions and energies to eliminate everything else. It empowered everyone on the team, however junior, to push back and say, "But does this new idea really help us to achieve our intent?" And it enabled them to better harness the support of partners to massively accelerate the journey. And even though their full aspiration isn't yet reached, that clarity of purpose enabled them to make a far greater contribution than they could have made under any other circumstances.

This is the kind of statement of purpose that we need for our companies, teams, and careers. So how do we craft a statement of purpose that is both concrete *and* inspiring, meaningful and memorable?

STOP WORDSMITHING AND START DECIDING

When developing statements of purpose – for your company, your team, or even yourself – there is a tendency to start obsessing about trivial stylistic details, like "Should we use this word or that word?" But this makes it all too easy to slip into meaningless clichés and buzzwords that lead to vague, meaningless statements like the ones I cited at the beginning of the chapter. An essential intent doesn't have to be elegantly crafted; it's the substance, not the style that counts. Instead, ask the more essential question that will inform every future decision you will ever make: "If we could be truly excellent at only one thing, what would it be?"

ASK, "HOW WILL WE KNOW WHEN WE'RE DONE?"

That said, when it comes to achieving clarity of purpose, inspiration does matter. When we think of inspiration, we often think of lofty rhetoric. But while rhetoric can certainly inspire, we need to remember that concrete objectives have the power to elevate and inspire as well. A powerful essential intent inspires people partially because it is concrete enough to answer the question, "How will we know when we have succeeded?"

This was illustrated brilliantly to me by Professor Bill Meehan, who spent thirty years with McKinsey advising CEOs and senior leaders on strategy and now teaches a class called "The Strategic Management of Nonprofits" at the Stanford School of Business. When I took his course as a postgraduate, one of the assignments he gave us was to evaluate the vision and mission statements of nonprofit organisations.

As the class reviewed more than one hundred examples, they noticed that some of the most grandiose were actually the *least* inspiring. For example, one had the mission to "eliminate hunger in the world," but given that there were just five people in the organisation, the mission felt like little more than empty words. Then out of the cluttered landscape of such loose idealism came a statement we all immediately understood and were inspired by. It was from a slightly unexpected place: the actor/social entrepreneur Brad Pitt, who, appalled by the lack of progress in rebuilding New Orleans after Hurricane Katrina, had started an organisation called "Make It Right" with the essential intent "to build 150 affordable, green, storm-resistant homes for families living in the Lower 9th Ward." That statement took the air out of the room. The concreteness of the objective made it real. The realness made it inspiring. It answered the question: "How will we know when we have succeeded?"

Living with Intent

Essential intent applies to so much more than your job description or your company's mission statement; a true essential intent is one that guides your greater sense of purpose, and helps you chart your life's path. For example, Nelson Mandela spent twenty-seven years in jail becoming an Essentialist. When he was thrown in jail in

1962 he had almost everything taken from him: his home, his reputation, his pride, and of course his freedom. He chose to use those twenty-seven years to focus on what was really essential and eliminate everything else – including his own resentment. He made it his essential intent to eliminate apartheid in South Africa and in doing so established a legacy that lives on today.

Creating an essential intent is hard. It takes courage, insight, and foresight to see which activities and efforts will add up to your single highest point of contribution. It takes asking tough questions, making real trade-offs, and exercising serious discipline to cut out the competing priorities that distract us from our true intention. Yet it is worth the effort because only with real clarity of purpose can people, teams, and organisations fully mobilise and achieve something truly excellent.

CHAPTER 11

DARE

The Power of a Graceful "No"

COURAGE IS GRACE UNDER PRESSURE.

—*Ernest Hemingway*

The right "no" spoken at the right time can change the course of history.

In just one example of many, Rosa Parks's quiet but resolute refusal to give up her seat on a segregated Montgomery, Alabma bus at exactly the right moment coalesced into forces that propelled the civil rights movement. As Parks recalled, "When [the bus driver] saw me still sitting, he asked if I was going to stand up, and I said, 'No, I'm not.'"[1]

Contrary to popular belief, her courageous "no" did not grow out of a particularly assertive tendency or personality in general. In fact, when she was made a secretary to the president of the Montgomery chapter of the NAACP she explained, "I was the only woman there, and they needed a secretary, and I was too timid to say no."[2]

Rather, her decision on the bus grew out of a deep conviction about what deliberate choice she wanted to make at that moment.

When the bus driver ordered her out of her seat, she said, "I felt a determination cover my body like a quilt on a winter night."[3] She did not know how her decision would spark a movement with reverberations around the world. But she *did* know her own mind. She knew, even as she was being arrested, that "it was the very last time that I would ever ride in humiliation of this kind."[4] Avoiding that humiliation was worth the risk of incarceration. Indeed, to her, it was essential.

It is true that we are (hopefully) unlikely to find ourselves facing a situation like that faced by Rosa Parks. Yet we can be inspired by her. We can think of her when we need the courage to dare to say no. We can remember her strength of conviction when we need to stand our ground in the face of social pressure to capitulate to the non-essential.

Have you ever felt a tension between what you felt was right and what someone was pressuring you to do? Have you ever felt the conflict between your internal conviction and an external action? Have you ever said yes when you meant no simply to avoid conflict or friction? Have you ever felt too scared or timid to turn down an invitation or request from a boss, colleague, friend, neighbour, or family member for fear of disappointing them? If you have, you're not alone. Navigating these moments with courage and grace is one of the most important skills to master in becoming an Essentialist – and one of the hardest.

I did not set out to write a chapter about courage. But the deeper I have looked at the subject of Essentialism the more clearly I have seen courage as key to the process of elimination. Without courage, the disciplined pursuit of less is just lip service. It is just the stuff of one more dinner party conversation. It is skin deep. Anyone can talk about the importance of focusing on the things that matter most – and many people do – but to see people who dare to live it is rare.

I say this without judgment. We have good reasons to fear saying no. We worry we'll miss out on a great opportunity. We're scared of rocking the boat, stirring things up, burning bridges. We can't bear the thought of disappointing someone we respect and like. None of this makes us a bad person. It's a natural part of being human. Yet as hard as it can be to say no to someone, failing to do so can cause us to miss out on something far more important.

A woman named Cynthia once told me a story about the time her father had made plans to take her on a night out in San Francisco. Twelve-year-old Cynthia and her father had been planning the "date" for months. They had a whole itinerary planned down to the minute: she would attend the last hour of his presentation, and then meet him at the back of the room at about four-thirty and leave quickly before everyone tried to talk to him. They would catch a tram to Chinatown, eat Chinese food (their favourite), shop for a souvenir, see the sights for a while and then "catch a flick" as her dad liked to say. Then they would grab a taxi back to the hotel, jump in the pool for a quick swim (her dad was famous for sneaking in when the pool was closed), order a hot fudge sundae from room service, and watch the late, late show. They discussed the details over and over again before they left. The anticipation was part of the whole experience.

This was all going according to plan until, as her father was leaving the convention centre, he ran into an old college friend and business associate. It had been years since they had seen each other, and Cynthia watched as they embraced enthusiastically. His friend said, in effect: "I am so glad you are doing some work with our company now. When Lois and I heard about it we thought it would be perfect. We want to invite you, and of course Cynthia, to get a spectacular seafood dinner down at the Wharf!" Cynthia's father responded: "Bob, it's so great to see you. Dinner at the wharf sounds great!"

Cynthia was crestfallen. Her daydreams of tram rides and ice cream sundaes evaporated in an instant. Plus, she hated seafood and she could just imagine how bored she would be listening to the adults talk all night. But then her father continued: "But not tonight. Cynthia and I have a special date planned, don't we?" He winked at Cynthia and grabbed her hand and they ran out of the door and continued with what was an unforgettable night in San Francisco.

As it happens, Cynthia's father was the management thinker Stephen R. Covey (author of *The Seven Habits of Highly Effective People*) who had passed away only weeks before Cynthia told me this story. So it was with deep emotion she recalled that evening in San Francisco. His simple decision "Bonded him to me forever because I knew what mattered most to him was me!" she said.[5]

Stephen R. Covey, one of the most respected and widely read business thinkers of his generation, was an Essentialist. Not only did he routinely teach Essentialist principles – like "The main thing is to keep the main thing the main thing" – to important leaders and heads of state around the world, he lived them.[6] And in this moment of living them with his daughter he made a memory that literally outlasted his lifetime. Seen with some perspective, his decision seems obvious. But many in his shoes would have accepted the friend's invitation for fear of seeming rude or ungrateful, or passing up a rare opportunity to dine with an old friend. So why is it so hard *in the moment* to dare to choose what is essential over what is non-essential?

One simple answer is we are unclear about what is essential. When this happens we become defenceless. On the other hand, when we have strong internal clarity it is almost as if we have a force field protecting us from the non-essentials coming at us from all directions. With Rosa it was her deep moral clarity that gave her unusual courage of conviction. With Stephen it was the clarity of his vision for the evening with his loving daughter. In virtually every instance, clarity about what is essential fuels us with the strength to say no to the non-essentials.

Essentially Awkward

A second reason why it is hard to choose what is essential in the moment is as simple as an innate fear of social awkwardness. The fact is, we as humans are wired to want to get along with others. After all, thousands of years ago when we all lived in tribes of hunter gatherers, our survival depended on it. And while conforming to what people in a group expect of us – what psychologists call normative conformity – is no longer a matter of life and death, the desire is still deeply ingrained in us.[7] This is why, whether it's an old friend who invites you to dinner or a boss who asks you to take on an important and high-profile project, or a neighbour who begs you to help with the school cake sale, the very thought of saying no literally brings us physical discomfort. We feel guilty. We don't want to let someone down. We are worried about damaging the relationship. But these emotions muddle our clarity. They distract us from the reality of the fact that either we can say no and regret it for a few minutes, or we can say yes and regret it for days, weeks, months, or even years.

The only way out of this trap is to learn to say no firmly, resolutely, and yet gracefully. Because once we do, we find, not only that our fears of disappointing or angering others were exaggerated, but that people actually respect us *more*. Since becoming an Essentialist I have found it almost universally true that people respect and admire those with the courage of conviction to say no.

Peter Drucker, in my view the father of modern management thinking, was also a master of the art of the graceful no. When Mihaly Csikszentmihalyi, the Hungarian professor most well known for his work on "flow," reached out to interview a series of creative individuals for a book he was writing on creativity, Drucker's response was interesting enough to Mihaly that he quoted it verbatim: "I am greatly honored and flattered by your kind letter of February 14th – for I have admired you and your work for many years, and I have learned much from it. But, my dear Professor Csikszentmihalyi, I am afraid I have to disappoint you. I could not possibly answer your questions. I am told I am creative – I don't know what that means. . . . I just keep on plodding. . . . I hope you will not think me presumptuous or rude if I say that one of the secrets of productivity (in which I believe whereas I do not believe in creativity) is to have a VERY BIG waste paper basket to take care of ALL invitations such as yours – productivity in my experience consists of NOT doing anything that helps the work of other people but to spend all one's time on the work the Good Lord has fitted one to do, and to do well."[8]

A true Essentialist, Peter Drucker believed that "people are effective because they say no."

Non-Essentialists say yes because of feelings of social awkwardness and pressure. They say yes automatically, without thinking, often in pursuit of the rush one gets from having pleased someone. But Essentialists know that after the rush comes the pang of regret. They know they will soon feel bullied and resentful – both at the other person and at themselves. Eventually they will wake up to the unpleasant reality that something more important must now be sacrificed to accommodate this new commitment. Of course, the point is not to say no to all requests. The point is to say no to the non-essentials so we can say yes to the things that really matter. It is to say no – frequently and gracefully – to everything *but* what is truly vital.

Non-Essentialist	Essentialist
Avoids saying no to avoid feeling social awkwardness and pressure	Dares to say no firmly, resolutely, and gracefully
Says yes to everything	Says yes only to the things that really matter

So how do we learn to say no gracefully? Below are general guidelines followed by a number of specific scripts for delivering the graceful "no."

SEPARATE THE DECISION FROM THE RELATIONSHIP

When people ask us to do something, we can confuse the request with our relationship with them. Sometimes they seem so interconnected, we forget that denying the request is not the same as denying the *person*. Only once we separate the decision from the relationship can we make a clear decision and then separately find the courage and compassion to communicate it.[9]

SAYING "NO" GRACEFULLY DOESN'T HAVE TO MEAN USING THE WORD *NO*

Essentialists *choose* "no" more often than they *say* no. There may be a time when the most graceful way to say no is to simply say a blunt *no*. But whether it's "I am flattered that you thought of me but I'm afraid I don't have the bandwidth" or "I would very much like to but I'm overcommitted," there are a variety of ways of refusing someone clearly and politely without actually using the word *no*. Later in the chapter you'll find more examples of ways to word your "no" gracefully.

FOCUS ON THE TRADE-OFF

The more we think about what we are giving up when we say yes to someone, the easier it is to say no. If we have no clear sense of the opportunity cost – in other words, the value of what we are giving up – then it is especially easy to fall into the non-essential trap of telling ourselves we can get it all done. We can't. A graceful "no" grows out of a clear but unstated calculation of the trade-off.

REMIND YOURSELF THAT EVERYONE IS SELLING SOMETHING

This doesn't mean you have to be cynical about people. I don't mean to imply people shouldn't be trusted. I am simply saying everyone is selling something – an idea, a viewpoint, an opinion – in exchange for your time. Simply being aware of what is being sold allows us to be more deliberate in deciding whether we want to buy it.

MAKE YOUR PEACE WITH THE FACT THAT SAYING "NO" OFTEN REQUIRES TRADING POPULARITY FOR RESPECT

When you say no, there is usually a short-term impact on the relationship. After all, when someone asks for something and doesn't get it, his or her immediate reaction may be annoyance or disappointment or even anger. This downside is clear. The potential upside, however, is less obvious: when the initial annoyance or disappointment or anger wears off, the respect kicks in. When we push back effectively, it shows people that our time is highly valuable. It distinguishes the professional from the amateur.

A case in point is the time the graphic designer Paul Rand had the guts to say no to Steve Jobs.[10] When Jobs was looking for a logo for the company NeXT, he asked Rand, whose work included the logos for IBM, UPS, Enron, Westinghouse, and ABC, to come up with a few options. But Rand didn't want to come up with "a few options." He wanted to design just one option. So Rand said: "No. I will solve your problem for you. And you will pay me. And you don't have to use the solution. If you want options go and talk to other people. But I will solve the problem the best way I know how. And you use it or not. That's up to you." Not surprisingly, Rand solved the problem and created the "jewel" logo Jobs wanted, but the real lesson here is the effect Rand's "push back" had on Jobs, who later said of Rand, "He is one of the most professional people I have ever worked with: in the sense that he had thought through all of the formal relationship between a client and a professional such as himself." Rand took a risk when he said no. He bet a short-term popularity loss for a long-term gain in respect. And it paid off.

Essentialists accept they cannot be popular with everyone all of the time. Yes, saying no respectfully, reasonably, and gracefully can come at a short-term social cost. But part of living the way of the Essentialist is realising respect is far more valuable than popularity in the long run.

REMEMBER THAT A CLEAR "NO" CAN BE MORE GRACEFUL THAN A VAGUE OR NONCOMMITTAL "YES"

As anyone who has ever been on the receiving end of this situation knows, a clear "I am going to pass on this" is far better than not getting back to someone or stringing them along with some noncommittal answer like "I will try to make this work" or "I might be able to" when you know they can't. Being vague is not the same as being graceful, and delaying the eventual "no" will only make it that much harder – and the recipient that much more resentful.

The "No" Repertoire

Remember, Essentialists don't say no just occasionally. It is a part of their regular repertoire. To consistently say no with grace, then, it helps to have a variety of responses to call upon. Below are eight responses you can put in your "no" repertoire.

1. *The awkward pause.* Instead of being controlled by the threat of an awkward silence, own it. Use it as a tool. When a request comes to you (obviously this works only in person), just pause for a moment. Count to three before delivering your verdict. Or if you get a bit more bold, simply wait for the other person to fill the void.

2. *The soft "no" (or the "no but").* I recently received an e-mail inviting me to coffee. I replied: "I am consumed with writing my book right now :) But I would love to get together once the book is finished. Let me know if we can get together towards the end of the summer."

E-mail is also a good way to start practising saying "no but" because it gives you the chance to draft and redraft your "no" to make it as graceful as possible. Plus, many people find that the distance of e-mail reduces the fear of awkwardness.

3. *"Let me check my calendar and get back to you."* One leader I know found her time being hijacked by other people all day. A classic non-Essentialist, she was capable and smart and unable to say no, and as a result she soon became a "go to" person. People would run up to her and say, "Could you help with X project?" Meaning to be a good citizen, she said yes. But soon she felt burdened with all of these different agendas. Things changed for her when she learned to use a new phrase: "Let me check my calendar and get back to you." It gave her the time to pause and reflect and ultimately reply that she was regretfully unavailable. It enabled her to take back control of her own decisions rather than be rushed into a "yes" when she was asked.

4. Use e-mail automatic replies. It is totally natural and expected to get an autoresponse when someone is travelling or out of the office. Really, this is the most socially acceptable "no" there is. People aren't saying they don't want to reply to your e-mail, they're just saying they can't get back to you for a period of time. So why limit these to holidays? When I was writing this book I set an e-mail auto reply with the subject line "In Monk Mode." The e-mail said: "Dear Friends, I am currently working on a new book which has put enormous burdens on my time. Unfortunately, I am unable to respond in the manner I would like. For this, I apologise. – Greg." And guess what? People seemed to adapt to my temporary absence and non-responsiveness just fine.

5. Say, "Yes. What should I deprioritise?" Saying no to a senior leader at work is almost unthinkable, even laughable, for many people. However, when saying yes is going to compromise your ability to make the highest level of contribution to your work, it is also your obligation. In this case it is not only reasonable to say no, it is essential. One effective way to do that is to remind your superiors what you would be neglecting if you said yes and force them to grapple with the trade-off.

For example, if your manager comes to you and asks you to do X, you can respond with "Yes, I'm happy to make this the priority. Which of these other projects should I deprioritise to pay attention to this new project?" Or simply say, "I would want to do a great job, and given my other commitments I wouldn't be able to do a job I was proud of if I took this on."

I know a leader who received this response from a subordinate. There was no way he wanted to be responsible for disrupting this productive and organised employee, so he took the non-essential work project back and gave it to someone else who was less organised!

6. *Say it with humour.* I recently was asked by a friend to join him in training for a marathon. My response was simple: "Nope!" He laughed a little and said, "Ah, you practicse what you preach." Just goes to show how useful it is to have a reputation as an Essentialist!

7. *Use the words "You are welcome to X. I am willing to Y."* For example, "You are welcome to borrow my car. I am willing to make sure the keys are here for you." By this you are also saying, "I won't be able to drive you." You *are* saying what you will not do, but you are couching it in terms of what you are willing to do. This is a particularly good way to navigate a request you would like to support somewhat but cannot throw your full weight behind.

I particularly like this construct because it also expresses a respect for *the other person's* ability to choose, as well as your own. It reminds both parties of the choices they have.

8. *"I can't do it, but X might be interested."* It is tempting to think that our help is uniquely invaluable, but often people requesting something don't really care if we're the ones who help them – as long as they get the help.

Kay Krill, the CEO of Ann, Inc. (a.k.a. Ann Taylor and LOFT women's clothing retailers), used to have a terrible time saying no to social invitations. As a result, she would end up at networking events she had no interest in attending. She would find herself going to office parties and regretting it the moment she got there.

Then one day one of her mentors came to her and told her that she had to learn to jettison the people and things of her life that just didn't matter, and that doing so would allow her to put 100 per cent of her energy into the things that had meaning for her. That advice liberated her. Now she is able to pick and choose. With practice, politely declining an invitation has become easy for her. Kay explains:

"I say no very easily because I know what is important to me. I only wish that I learned how to do that earlier in my life."[11]

Saying no is its own leadership capability. It is not just a peripheral skill. As with any ability, we start with limited experience. We are novices at "no." Then we learn a couple of basic techniques. We make mistakes. We learn from them. We develop more skills. We keep practising. After a while we have a whole repertoire available at our disposal, and in time we have gained mastery of a type of social art form. We can handle almost any request from almost anybody with grace and dignity. Tom Friel, the former CEO of Heidrick & Struggles, once said to me, "We need to learn the slow 'yes' and the quick 'no.'"

CHAPTER 12

UNCOMMIT

Win Big by Cutting Your Losses

HALF OF THE TROUBLES OF THIS LIFE CAN BE
TRACED TO SAYING YES TOO QUICKLY AND
NOT SAYING NO SOON ENOUGH.

—*Josh Billings*

By any estimation, the Concorde jet was a striking achievement in aeronautical engineering. Aboard this passenger plane you could fly from London to New York in as little as two hours, fifty-two minutes, and fifty-nine seconds.[1] That's less than half the time of a traditional plane, making the Concorde the fastest passenger plane in the world.

Unfortunately, it was also an extraordinary financial failure. Of course many great ideas, innovations, and products are. But what made this one different was that it consistently lost money for *more than four decades*. Yet each time it went over budget the French and British governments poured more and more money in. They did this even knowing that the chance of recouping their continued investments, let alone the original expenditures, were miniscule; with the plane's limited seating, few orders coming in, and the high cost of production, it was clear that even with exaggerated estimates the project would never be profitable. Indeed, when the British cabinet papers were released under the thirty-year rule, they revealed that government ministers at the time knew the investment "could not stand on normal economic grounds."[2]

Why would intelligent, capable British and French government officials continue to invest in what was clearly a losing proposition for so long? One reason is a very common psychological phenomenon called "sunk-cost bias."

Sunk-cost bias is the tendency to continue to invest time, money, or energy into something we know is a losing proposition simply because we have already incurred, or sunk, a cost that cannot be recouped. But of course this can easily become a vicious cycle: the more we invest, the more determined we become to see it through and see our investment pay off. The more we invest in something, the harder it is to let go.

The sunk costs for developing and building the Concorde were around $1 billion. Yet the more money the British and French governments poured into it, the harder it was to walk away.[3] Individuals are equally vulnerable to sunk-cost bias. It explains why we'll continue to sit through a terrible movie because we've already paid the price of a ticket. It explains why we continue to pour money into a home renovation that never seems to near completion. It explains why we'll continue to wait for a bus or a subway train that never comes instead of hailing a cab, and it explains why we invest in toxic relationships even when our efforts only make things worse. Examples like this abound; consider the somewhat bizarre story of an American named Henry Gribbohm, who recently spent his entire life savings, $2,600 in total, at a carnival game trying to win an Xbox. The more he spent, the more determined he became to win. Henry said, "You just get caught up in the whole 'I've got to win my money back,' but it didn't turn out that way."[4] The more he invested in trying to win this utterly non-essential item, the harder it was for him to walk away.

Have you ever continued to invest time or effort in a non-essential project instead of cutting your losses? Have you ever continued to pour money into an investment that wasn't panning out instead of walking away? Have you ever kept plodding down a dead end because you could not admit, "I shouldn't have pursued this direction in the first place"? Ever been stuck in a cycle of "throwing good money after bad"? A non-Essentialist can't break free of traps like these. An Essentialist has the courage and confidence to admit his or her mistakes and uncommit, no matter the sunk costs.

Non-Essentialist	Essentialist
Asks, "Why stop now when I've already invested so much in this project?"	Asks, "If I weren't already invested in this project, how much would I invest in it now?"
Thinks, "If I just keep trying, I can make this work."	Thinks, "What else could I do with this time or money if I pulled the plug now?"
Hates admitting to mistakes	Comfortable with cutting losses

Sunk-cost bias, while all too common, isn't the only non-Essentialist trap to watch out for. Below are several other common traps and tips for how to extricate yourself politely, gracefully, and with minimal cost.

Avoiding Commitment Traps

BEWARE OF THE ENDOWMENT EFFECT

A sense of ownership is a powerful thing. As the saying goes, nobody in the history of the world has washed their hire car! This is because of something called "the endowment effect," our tendency to undervalue things that aren't ours and to overvalue things because we already own them.

In one study demonstrating the power of the endowment effect, the Nobel Prize-winning researcher Daniel Kahneman and colleagues randomly gave coffee mugs to only half the subjects in an experiment.[5] The first group was asked how much they would be willing to sell their mug for, while the second group was asked what they would be willing to pay for it. It turned out the students who "owned" the mugs refused to sell for less than $5.25, while those without the cups were willing to pay only $2.25 to $2.75. The mere fact of ownership, in other words, caused the mug owners to value the objects more highly and made them less willing to part with them.

In your own life, I'm sure you can think of items that seem to be more valuable the moment you think about giving them away. Think of a book on your shelf you haven't read in years, or a kitchen appliance still sitting in the box, or the sweater you got from Aunt Mildred but never wore. Whether or not you get any use or enjoyment out of them, subconsciously, the very fact that they are yours makes you value them more highly than you would if they didn't belong to you.

Unfortunately, we have this bias when it comes to non-essential activities as well as belongings. The project that isn't getting anywhere at work seems that much more critical when we're the team leader on it. The commitment to volunteer at the local cake sale becomes harder to get out of when we're the one who put the fund-raiser together. When we feel we "own" an activity, it becomes harder to uncommit. Nonetheless, here is a useful tip:

PRETEND YOU DON'T OWN IT YET

Tom Stafford describes a simple antidote to the endowment effect.[6] Instead of asking, "How much do I value this item?" we should ask, "If I did not own this item, how much would I pay to obtain it?" We can do the same for opportunities and commitment. Don't ask, "How will I feel if I miss out on this opportunity?" but rather, "If I did not have this opportunity, how much would I be willing to sacrifice in order to obtain it?" Similarly, we can ask, "If I wasn't already involved in this project, how hard would I work to get on it?"[7]

GET OVER THE FEAR OF WASTE

Hal Arkes, a professor of psychology at Ohio State University who studies judgment in decision making, was puzzled by an enigma. Why are adults so much more vulnerable to the sunk-cost bias than young children? The answer, he believes, is a lifetime of exposure to the "Don't waste" rule, so that by the time we are adults we are trained to avoid appearing wasteful, even to ourselves.[8] "Abandoning a project that you've invested a lot in feels like you've wasted everything, and waste is something we're told to avoid," Arkes said.[9]

To illustrate this he gave the following scenario to a group of participants: "Assume that you have spent $100 on a ticket for a weekend ski trip to Michigan. Several weeks later you buy a $50 ticket for a weekend ski trip to Wisconsin. You think you will enjoy the Wisconsin ski trip more than the Michigan ski trip. As you are putting your newly purchased Wisconsin ticket in your wallet you notice that the Michigan ski trip and the Wisconsin ski trip are for the same weekend. It's too late to sell or return either ticket. You must choose which to use." When asked, "Which ski trip will you go on?" more than half said they would opt for the more expensive trip, even though they would enjoy it less. Their (faulty) reasoning was that using the cheaper ticket would be wasting more money than using the expensive ticket. It's natural not to want to let go of what we wasted on a bad choice, but when we don't, we doom ourselves to keep wasting even more.

INSTEAD, ADMIT FAILURE TO BEGIN SUCCESS

I remember a friend who would never stop to ask for directions because he could never admit he was lost. So we would waste time and energy driving around in circles, getting nowhere – the epitome of a non-essential activity.

Only when we admit we have made a mistake in committing to something can we make a mistake a part of our past. When we remain in denial, on the other hand, we continue to circle pointlessly. There should be no shame in admitting to a mistake; after all, we really are only admitting that we are now wiser than we once were.

STOP TRYING TO FORCE A FIT

In the movie *Tootsie,* Dustin Hoffman plays a struggling actor who is trying to get work. The movie begins comically with a series of failed auditions. At one he is told, "We need someone a little older." At the next he is told, "We're looking for someone younger." Then at the next, "You're the wrong height," to which he responds, "I can be taller." The executive responds, "No. We're looking for somebody shorter." Desperate to make it work, Hoffman's character explains: "Look. I don't have to be this tall. See, I'm wearing lifts. I can be shorter." But the executive also insists, "I know, but we're looking for somebody different." Still persistent, the would-be actor pushes back again: "I can be different." The point is that we often act like Dustin Hoffman's character by trying too hard to be something we're not. Whether in our personal or professional lives, it is all too tempting to force something that is simply a mismatch. The solution?

GET A NEUTRAL SECOND OPINION

When we get so emotionally hung up on trying to force something that is not the right fit, we can often benefit from a sounding board. Someone who is not emotionally involved in the situation and unaffected by the choice we make can give us the permission to stop forcing something that is clearly not working out.

I once wasted months of effort trying to force a project that just wasn't working out. Looking back, the more I put into it the worse things became. But my irrational response was to invest still more. I thought, "I can make this work!" I did not want to accept I had been wasting my effort. I finally shared my frustration with a friend who had the advantage of being emotionally removed from the project – someone who wasn't burdened with the sunk costs and could evaluate my decisions with some perspective. After listening to me he said, "You're not married to this." And with those simple words I was liberated to stop investing in a non-essential.

BE AWARE OF THE STATUS QUO BIAS

The tendency to continue doing something simply because we have always done it is sometimes called the "status quo bias." I once worked at a company that used an employee evaluation system that seemed to me so woefully outdated that I became curious about how long it had been in place. As I searched for its creator in the company I found that nobody, up to and including the long-standing head of HR, knew of its origin. More shocking still, in the ten years she had been at the company, nobody had once questioned the system. It's all too easy to blindly accept and not bother to question commitments simply because they have already been established.

One cure for the status quo bias is borrowed from the world of accounting:

APPLY ZERO-BASED BUDGETING

Typically, when accountants allocate a budget they use last year's budget as the baseline for the next year's projection. But with zero-based budgeting, they use zero as the baseline. In other words, every item in the proposed budget must be justified from scratch. While this takes more effort it has many advantages: it efficiently allocates resources on the basis of needs rather than history, it detects exaggerated budget requests, it draws attention to obsolete operations, and it encourages people to be clearer in their purpose and how their expenses align to that project.

You can apply zero-based budgeting to your own endeavours. Instead of trying to budget your time on the basis of existing commitments, assume that all bets are off. All previous commitments are gone. Then begin from scratch, asking which you would add today. You can do this with everything from the financial obligations you have to projects you are committed to, even relationships you are in. Every use of time, energy, or resources has to justify itself anew. If it no longer fits, eliminate it altogether.

STOP MAKING CASUAL COMMITMENTS

Some people's days are full to the brim with soft commitments they have taken on unintentionally through an offhand comment or casual conversation they had somewhere with someone. You know the kind I mean – you're chatting with your neighbour about her work on the PTA, your colleague about a new initiative she is heading, or your friend about a new restaurant he wants to try, and before you know it, boom, you're committed.

FROM NOW ON, PAUSE BEFORE YOU SPEAK

It might sound obvious, but pausing for just five seconds before offering your services can greatly reduce the possibility of making a commitment you'll regret. Before the words "That sounds great, I'd love to" fly out of your mouth, ask yourself, "Is this essential?" If you've already made a casual commitment you're regretting, find a nice way to worm your way out. Simply apologise and tell the person that when you made the commitment you didn't fully realise what it would entail.

GET OVER THE FEAR OF MISSING OUT

We've seen ample evidence in this chapter suggesting that the majority of us are naturally very loss-averse. As a result, one of the obstacles to uncommitting ourselves from a present course is the fear of missing out on something great.

TO FIGHT THIS FEAR, RUN A REVERSE PILOT

One of the ideas that has grown popular in business circles in recent years is "prototyping." Building a prototype, or large-scale model, allows companies to test-run an idea or product without making a huge investment up front. Exactly the same idea can be used in reverse to eliminate non-essentials in a relatively low-risk way, by running what Daniel Shapero, a director at LinkedIn, calls a "reverse pilot."[10]

In a reverse pilot you test whether *removing* an initiative or activity will have any negative consequences. For example, when an executive I work with took on a new senior role in the company, he inherited a process his predecessor had gone to a huge effort to implement: a huge, highly visual report on a myriad of subjects produced for the other executives each week. It consumed enormous energy from his team, and he hypothesised that it was not adding a great deal of value to the company. So to test his hypothesis he ran a reverse pilot. He simply stopped publishing the report and waited to see what the response would be. What he found was that no one seemed to miss it; after several weeks nobody had even mentioned the report. As a result, he concluded that the report was not essential to the business and could be eliminated.

A similar reverse pilot can be carried out in our social lives. Are there commitments you routinely make to customers, colleagues, friends or even family members that you have always assumed made a big difference to them but that in fact they might barely notice? By quietly eliminating or at least scaling back an activity for a few days or weeks you might be able to assess whether it is *really* making a difference or whether no one really cares.

Even using these techniques, it's true that "uncommitting" can be harder than simply not committing in the first place. We feel guilty saying no to something or someone we have already committed to, and let's face it, no one likes going back on their word. Yet learning how to do so – in ways that will garner you respect for your courage, focus, and discipline – is crucial to becoming an Essentialist.

CHAPTER 13

EDIT

The Invisible Art

I SAW THE ANGEL IN THE MARBLE AND CARVED
UNTIL I SET HIM FREE.

—Michelangelo

Every year at The Oscars the most notable prize is for "Best Picture."
The media speculate on it for weeks prior to the broadcast, and most
viewers stay up well past their bedtimes to see it awarded. There is
a far less hyped award on the night: the one for film editing. Let's
face it: most viewers switch the channel or go into the kitchen to
refill their popcorn bowl when the winner of "Best Film Editing"
is announced. Yet what most people don't know is that the two
awards are highly correlated: since 1981 not a single film has won
Best Picture without at least being nominated for Film Editing. In
fact, in about two-thirds of the cases the movie nominated for Film
Editing has gone on to win Best Picture.[1]

In the history of The Oscars the most respected (if not exactly
celebrated) film editor is Michael Kahn, with eight nominations
– more than anyone else in the business – and three wins under
his belt. While his is hardly a household name, the films he has
edited certainly are. He is the editor of such notable films as

Saving Private Ryan, Raiders of the Lost Ark, Schindler's List, and *Lincoln.* Indeed, over thirty-seven years he has edited almost all of Steven Spielberg's movies, becoming his right-hand man in the process. Yet only a handful of people know Kahn's name. It is for good reason that film editing is sometimes known as the "invisible art."

Clearly, editing – which involves the strict elimination of the trivial, unimportant, or irrelevant – is an Essentialist craft. So what makes a good editor? When the editing branch of the Academy of Motion Picture Arts and Sciences sits down to select their Oscar nominees for film editing, they try, as Mark Harris has written, "very hard not to look at what they're supposed to be looking at."[2] In other words, a good film editor makes it hard *not* to see what's important because she eliminates everything but the elements that absolutely need to be there.

In chapter 6 we likened exploring to being a journalist; it involves asking questions, listening, and connecting the dots in order to distinguish the essential few from the trivial many. So it makes sense that the next stage in the Essentialist process, eliminating the non-essentials, means taking on the role of an editor in your life and leadership.

Jack Dorsey is best known as the creator of Twitter and as the founder and CEO of Square, a mobile payments company. His Essentialist approach to management is a relatively rare one. At a dinner I attended recently where he spoke, he said he thinks of the role of CEO as being the chief editor of the company. At another event at Stanford University he explained further: "By editorial I mean there are a thousand things we could be doing. But there [are] only one or two that are important. And all of these ideas . . . and inputs from engineers, support people, designers are going to constantly flood what we should be doing. . . . As an editor I am constantly taking these inputs and deciding the one, or intersection of a few, that make sense for what we are doing."[3]

An editor is not merely someone who says no to things. A three-year-old can do that. Nor does an editor simply eliminate; in fact, in a way, an editor actually *adds*. What I mean is that a good editor is someone who uses *deliberate subtraction* to actually add life to the ideas, setting, plot, and characters.

Likewise, in life, disciplined editing can help add to your level of contribution. It increases your ability to focus on and give energy to the things that really matter. It lends the most meaningful relationships and activities more space to blossom.

Editing aids the effortless execution of the Essentialist by removing anything distracting or unnecessary or awkward. Or, as one book editor put it: "My job is to make life as effortless as possible for the reader. The goal is to help the reader have the clearest possible understanding of the most important message."

Of course, editing also involves making trade-offs. Instead of trying to fit it all in – every character, every plot twist, every detail – an editor asks, "Will this character or plot twist or detail make it better?" For an author – whether of films, books, or journalism – it is easy to get overly committed to a certain idea or body of work, especially one you slaved over. It can be quite painful to eliminate passages, pages, or even chapters that took weeks, months, maybe even years to write in the first place. Yet such disciplined elimination is critical to the craft. You must, as Stephen King has said, "kill your darlings, kill your darlings, even when it breaks your egocentric little scribbler's heart, kill your darlings."[4]

Non-Essentialist	Essentialist
Thinks that making things better means adding something	Thinks that making things better means subtracting something
Attached to every word, image, or detail	Eliminates the distracting words, images, and details

Of course, editing a film, or a book, or any other creative work is not the same as editing your life. In life, we don't have the luxury of revisiting a conversation we have just had, or a meeting we just led, or a presentation we just made and reworking it, red pen in hand. Nevertheless, four simple principles inherent in editing do apply to editing the non-essentials out of our lives.

Editing Life

CUT OUT OPTIONS

To state the obvious, editing involves cutting out things that confuse the reader and cloud the message or story. It is a matter of record that well-edited movies and books are easy on the eye and the brain.

When making decisions, deciding to cut options can be terrifying – but the truth is, it is the very essence of decision making.[5] In fact:

The Latin root of the word *decision – cis* or *cid* – literally means "to cut" or "to kill."

You can see this in words like *scissors, homicide,* or *fratricide.* Since ultimately, having fewer options actually makes a decision "easier on the eye and the brain," we must summon the discipline to get rid of options or activities that may be good, or even really good, but that get in the way. Yes, making the choice to eliminate something good can be painful. But eventually, every cut produces joy – maybe not in the moment but afterwards, when we realise that every additional moment we have gained can be spent on something better. That may be one reason why Stephen King has written, "To write is human, to edit is divine."[6]

CONDENSE

Many people have been credited with coming up with this apt sentiment: "I must apologise: if I had more time I would have written a shorter letter." It's true that doing less can be harder, both in art and in life. Every word, every scene, every activity must count for more. An editor is ruthless in the pursuit of making every word count. Instead of saying it in two sentences, can you say it in one? Is it possible to use one word where two are currently being used? As Alan D. Williams observed in the essay "What Is an Editor?" there are "two basic questions the editor should be addressing to the author: Are you saying what you want to say? and, Are you saying it as clearly and concisely as possible?"[7] Condensing means saying it as clearly and concisely as possible.

Likewise, in life, condensing allows us to do more with less. For example, when Graham Hill moved into a 420-square-foot apartment in New York, he wanted to see how well he could condense everything he owned. The ultimate result was a design he calls a "little jewel box." The jewel box works because every piece of furniture has multiple functions. The wall on the left, for example, acts as a large projector screen for watching movies and also houses two guest beds that can be pulled out when visitors come to stay. The wall to the right folds down, over the couch, to reveal a queen bed. Everything does double or triple duty; in other words, everything makes a greater contribution to apartment life. This design turned out to be so innovative that he turned it into a business devoted to the art of getting more out of less space. He named it, appropriately, LifeEdited.com.

But to be clear, condensing doesn't mean doing more at once, it simply means less waste. It means lowering the ratio of words to ideas, square feet to usefulness, or effort to results. Thus to apply the principle of condensing to our lives we need to shift the ratio of activity to meaning. We need to eliminate multiple meaningless activities and replace them with one very meaningful activity. For example, one employee at a company I've worked with (one who was well enough established to not have to worry about being fired) routinely skipped the weekly meeting other people attended and would simply ask them what he had missed. Thus he condensed a two-hour meeting into ten minutes and invested the rest of that redeemed time getting the important work done.

CORRECT

An editor's job is not just to cut or condense but also to make something right. It can be a change as minor as a grammar correction or as involved as fixing the flaws in an argument. To do this well, an editor must have a clear sense of the overarching purpose of the work he or she is editing. As Michael Kahn explains, he doesn't always do what Spielberg tells him to do; instead, he does what he thinks Spielberg really wants. Understanding the overarching intent allows him to make the corrections that even Spielberg himself might not be able to verbalise.

Similarly, in our own professional or private lives we can make corrections by coming back to our core purpose. Having a clear overarching intent, as discussed in chapter 10, enables us to check ourselves – to regularly compare our activities or behaviours to our real intent. If they are incorrect, we can edit them.

EDIT LESS

This may seem a little counterintuitive. But the best editors don't feel the need to change everything. They know that sometimes having the discipline to leave certain things exactly as they are is the best use of their editorial judgment. It is just one more way in which being an editor is an invisible craft. The best surgeon is not the one

who makes the most incisions; similarly, the best editors can sometimes be the least intrusive, the most restrained.

Becoming an editor in our lives also includes knowing when
to show restraint. One way we can do this is by editing our tendency to step in. When we are added onto an e-mail thread, for
example, we can resist our usual temptation to be the first to "reply
all". When sitting in a meeting, we can resist the urge to add our
two cents. We can wait. We can observe. We can see how things
develop. Doing less is not just a powerful Essentialist strategy, it's a
powerful editorial one as well.

A non-Essentialist views editing as a discrete task to be performed
only when things become overwhelming. But waiting too long to
edit will force us to make major cuts not always of our choosing.
Editing our time and activities continuously allows us to make
more minor but deliberate adjustments along the way. Becoming
an Essentialist means making cutting, condensing, and correct-
ing a natural part of our daily routine – making editing a natural
cadence in our lives.

CHAPTER 14

LIMIT

The Freedom of Setting Boundaries

NO IS A COMPLETE SENTENCE.

—*Anne Lamott*

Jin-Yung[1] was an employee of a technology company in Korea who found herself planning her wedding while simultaneously preparing for a board meeting that was to take place three weeks prior to her big day. When her manager, Hyori, asked Jin-Yung to create the script and all the slides for their joint presentation at the board meeting, Jin-Yung put in several fifteen-hour days and completed the work quickly so she could devote the days leading up to the board meeting to planning her wedding. Her manager was surprised and delighted that the work was done ahead of schedule, and Jin-Yung was now free to immerse herself in five uninterrupted days of wedding planning.

Then Jin-Yung received an urgent request from her manager asking her to complete an additional project prior to the board meeting. In their several years of working together, Jin-Yung had never said "No" to Hyori, even when saying yes threw her life into temporary turmoil (as it often did). Up to this point, Jin-Yung had given unknowable hours to executing every request and task, and delivering them in neat and complete packages, no matter the sacrifice. This time, however, she did not hesitate and she said "No" to her manager. She chose not to apologise or overjustify her answer. She simply said, "I have planned for this time, I have worked hard for it and I deserve to have it . . . guilt-free!"

Then something shocking happened. Everyone else in the team said "No" and Hyori, the manager, was left to complete the task on her own. At first, Hyori was fuming. It had taken her all week to complete the task, and she wasn't happy about it. But after labouring over the task for days, she saw all sorts of flaws in the way she'd been doing things. She soon realised that if she wanted to be a more effective manager, she needed to pull in the reins, and be clear with each member of the team about expectations, accountability, and outcomes. In the end, she was grateful to Jin-Yung for helping her see the error of her ways. By establishing boundaries, Jin-Yung not only opened her manager's eyes to unhealthy team dynamics and opened up a space for change, she did it in a way that earned her abiding gratitude and respect.

The disappearance of boundaries is typical of our non-Essentialist era. For one thing, of course, technology has completely blurred the lines between work and family. These days there don't seem to be any boundaries at all regarding when people expect us to be available to work. (I recently had an executive assistant provide me with times for a client meeting that included Saturday morning, even though there was no particular urgency for the meeting, and no acknowledgment that Saturday was an unusual day to offer. Has Saturday become the new Friday? I wondered.) But what most people don't realise is that the problem is not just that the boundaries have been *blurred*; it's that the boundary of work has edged insidiously into family territory. It is hard to imagine executives in most companies who would be comfortable with employees bringing their children to work on Monday morning, yet they seem to have no problem expecting their employees to come into the office or to work on a project on a Saturday or Sunday.

Clayton Christensen, the Harvard business professor and author of *The Innovator's Dilemma*, was once asked to make just such a sacrifice. At the time, he was working for a management consulting firm, and one of the partners came to him and told him he needed to come in on Saturday to help work on a project. Clay simply responded: "Oh, I am so sorry. I have made the commitment that every Saturday is a day to be with my wife and children."

The partner, displeased, stormed off, but later he returned and he said: "Clay, fine. I have talked with everyone on the team and they said they will come in on Sunday instead. So I will expect you to be there." Clay sighed and said: "I appreciate you trying to do that. But Sunday will not work. I have given Sunday to God and so I won't be able to come in." If the partner was frustrated before, he was much more so now.

Still, Clay was not fired for standing his ground, and while his choice was not popular in the moment, ultimately he was respected for it. The boundaries paid off.

Clay recalls: "That taught me an important lesson. If I had made an exception then I might have made it many times."[2] Boundaries are a little like the walls of a sandcastle. The second we let one fall over, the rest of them come crashing down.

I won't deny that setting boundaries can be hard. Just because it worked out for Jin-Yung and Clay doesn't mean it always does. Jin-Yung could have lost the job opportunity. Clay's unwillingness to work at weekends could have limited his career. It's true that boundaries can come at a high price.

However, not pushing back costs more: our ability to choose what is most essential in life. For Jin-Yung and Clay, respect in the workplace and time for God and family were most important, so these were the things they deliberately and strategically chose to prioritise. After all, if you don't set boundaries – there won't be any. Or even worse, there will be boundaries, but they'll be set by default – or by another person – instead of by design.

Non-Essentialists tend to think of boundaries as constraints or limits, things that get in the way of their hyperproductive life. To a non-Essentialist, setting boundaries is evidence of weakness. If they are strong enough, they think, they don't need boundaries. They can cope with it all. They can do it all. But without limits, they eventually become spread so thin that getting anything done becomes virtually impossible.

Essentialists, on the other hand, see boundaries as empowering. They recognise that boundaries protect their time from being hijacked and often free them from the burden of having to say no to things that further others' objectives instead of their own. They know that clear boundaries allow them to proactively eliminate the demands and encumbrances from others that distract them from the true essentials.

Non-Essentialist	Essentialist
Thinks if you have limits you will be limited	Knows that if you have limits you will become limitless
Sees boundaries as constraining	Sees boundaries as liberating
Exerts effort attempting the direct "no"	Sets rules in advance that eliminate the need for the direct "no"

Their Problem Is Not Your Problem

Of course, the challenge of setting boundaries goes far beyond the workplace. In our personal lives, too, there are some people who seem to know no boundaries when they make demands on our time. How often do you feel your Saturday or Sunday is being hijacked by someone else's agenda? Is there someone in your personal life who doesn't seem to sense when he or she is crossing the line?

We all have some people in our lives who tend to be higher maintenance for us than others. These are the people who make their problem our problem. They distract us from our purpose. They care only about their own agendas, and if we let them they prevent us from making our highest level of contribution by siphoning our time and energy off to activities that are essential to *them,* rather than those that are essential to us.

So how do we take a page from Jin-Yung and Clayton Christensen and set the kinds of boundaries that will protect us from other people's agendas? Below are several guidelines for your consideration.

DON'T ROB PEOPLE OF THEIR PROBLEMS

I am not saying we should never help people. We should serve, and love, and make a difference in the lives of others, of course. But when people make their problem our problem, we aren't helping them; we're enabling them. Once we take their problem for them, all we're doing is taking away their ability to solve it.

The author Henry Cloud tells a story about just this kind of situation in his book *Boundaries*. Once, the parents of a twenty-five-year-old man came to see Cloud. They wanted him to "fix" their son. He asked them why they had come without their son, and they said, "Well, he doesn't think he has a problem." After listening to their story Henry concluded, to their surprise: "I think your son is right. He doesn't have a problem. . . . You do. . . . You pay, you fret, you worry, you plan, you exert energy to keep him going. He doesn't have a problem because you have taken it from him."[3]

Cloud then offered them a metaphor. Imagine a neighbour who never waters his lawn. But whenever you turn on your sprinkler system, the water falls on his lawn. Your grass is turning brown and dying, but Bill looks down at his green grass and thinks to himself, "My garden is doing fine." Thus everyone loses: your efforts have been wasted, and Bill never develops the habit of watering his own lawn. The solution? As Cloud puts it, "You need some fences to keep his problems out of your garden and in his, where they belong."

In the working world, people try to use our sprinklers to water their own grass all the time. This may come in the form of a boss who puts you on a committee for her pet project, a colleague who asks for your input on a report or presentation or proposal she hasn't taken the time to perfect yet herself, or a colleague who stops you in the corridor and talks your ear off when you have an important meeting to get to or a vital phone call to make or critical work on your desk.

Whoever it is that's trying to siphon off your time and energies for their own purpose, the only solution is to put up fences. And not at the moment the request is made – you need to put up your fences well in advance, clearly demarcating what's off limits so you can head off time wasters and boundary pushers at the pass. Remember, forcing these people to solve their own problems is equally beneficial for you and for them.

BOUNDARIES ARE A SOURCE OF LIBERATION

This truth is demonstrated elegantly by the story of a school located next to a busy road. At first the children played only on a small swath of the playground, close to the building where the grown-ups could keep their eyes on them. But then someone constructed a fence around the playground. Now the children were able to play anywhere and everywhere in the playground. Their freedom, in effect, more than doubled.[4]

Similarly, when we don't set clear boundaries in our lives we can end up imprisoned by the limits others have set for us. When we have clear boundaries, on the other hand, we are free to select from the whole area – or the whole range of options – that *we* have deliberately chosen to explore.

FIND YOUR DEALBREAKERS

When I ask executives to identify their boundaries they can rarely do it. They know they have some, but they cannot put them into words. The simple reality is, if you can't articulate these to yourself and others, it may be unrealistic to expect other people to respect them or even figure them out.

Think of one person who frequently pulls you off your most essential path. Make a list of your dealbreakers – the types of requests or activities from that person that you simply refuse to say yes to unless they somehow overlap with your own priorities or agenda.

Another quick test for *finding* your dealbreakers is to write down any time you feel violated or put upon by someone's request. It doesn't have to be in some extreme way for you to notice it. Even a small "pinch" (to use a description I think is helpful for describing a minor violation of your boundaries) that makes you feel even a twinge of resentment – whether it's an unwanted invitation, an unsolicited "opportunity," or a request for a small favour – is a clue for discovering your own hidden boundaries.

CRAFT SOCIAL CONTRACTS

I was once paired with a colleague who approached projects in a completely opposite way. People predicted there would be fireworks between us. But our working relationship was actually quite harmonious. Why? Because when we first got together I made it a point to lay out my priorities and what extra work I would and wouldn't be willing to take on over the life span of the project. "Let's just agree on what we want to achieve," I began. "Here are a couple of things that really matter to me . . ." And I asked him to do the same.

Thus we worked through a "social contract," not unlike the one Jin-Yung and her boss worked out in the opening story. Simply having an understanding up front about what we were really trying to achieve and what our boundaries were kept us from wasting each other's time, saddling each other with burdensome requests, and distracting each other from the things that were essential to us. As a result, we were each able to make our highest level of contribution on the project – and we got along famously, despite our differences, throughout the process.

With practice, enforcing your limits will become easier and easier.

execute

HOW CAN WE MAKE DOING
THE VITAL FEW THINGS
ALMOST EFFORTLESS?

EXECUTE

How to Make Execution Effortless

There are two ways of thinking about execution.

While non-Essentialists tend to force execution, Essentialists invest the time they have saved by eliminating the non-essentials into designing a system to make execution almost effortless.

In chapter 1 we talked how our life can resemble an overly full wardrobe and how an Essentialist would approach organising it. We talked about how if you want your wardrobe to stay tidy you need a regular routine. You need to have one large bag for items you need to throw away and a very small pile for items you want to keep. You need to know the drop-off location and the hours of your local charity shop. You need to have a scheduled time to go there.

In other words, once you've figured out which activities and efforts to keep in your life, you have to have a system for executing them. You can't wait until that wardrobe is bursting at the seams and then take superhuman efforts to purge it. You have to have a system in place so that keeping it neat becomes routine and effortless.

It is human nature to want to do easy things. In this part of the book you'll learn how to make executing the right things — the essential things — as easy and frictionless as possible.

CHAPTER 15

BUFFER

The Unfair Advantage

GIVE ME SIX HOURS TO CHOP DOWN A TREE AND I WILL
SPEND THE FIRST FOUR SHARPENING THE AXE.

—Attributed to Abraham Lincoln

In the Hebrew Bible a story is told of Joseph (of *Amazing Technicolor Dreamcoat* fame), who saved Egypt from a savage, seven-year famine. The Pharaoh had a dream he could not interpret and asked his wisest advisers to explain it correctly to him. They couldn't interpret it either, but someone remembered that Joseph, who was in prison at the time, had a reputation for explaining the meaning of dreams, and thus he was called for.

In the dream Pharaoh was standing by a river when he saw seven "fat-fleshed" kine (or cows) come out of the water and feed in a meadow. Then seven others came out that were "lean-fleshed." The second set of cows ate the first set. Joseph explained that the dream meant there would be seven years of plenty in Egypt and then seven years of famine. Therefore, Joseph suggested that the Pharaoh appoint someone "discreet and wise" to take a fifth of the harvest every year for seven years and store it as a buffer for the years of famine. The plan was approved and Joseph was given the position of vizier, or second in command, over Egypt. He executed the plan perfectly so that when the seven years of famine arrived everyone in Egypt and the surrounding areas, including Joseph's extended family, was saved. In this simple story is one of the most powerful practices Essentialists employ to ensure effortless execution.

The reality is that we live in an unpredictable world. Even apart from extreme events such as famines, we face the unexpected constantly. We do not know whether the traffic will be clear or congested. We do not know if our flight will be delayed or cancelled. We do not know if we'll slip on an icy pavement tomorrow and break our wrist. Similarly, in the workplace we do not know if a supplier will be late, or a colleague will drop the ball, or a client will change his or her directions at the eleventh hour, and so on. The only thing we can expect (with any great certainty) is the unexpected. Therefore, we can either wait for the moment and react to it or we can prepare. We can create a buffer.

A "buffer" can be defined literally as something that prevents two things from coming into contact and harming each other. For example, a "buffer zone" at the periphery of a protected environmental area is an area of land that is used to create extra space between that area and any potential threats that might infiltrate it.

On one occasion I was trying to explain the concept of buffers to my children. We were in the car together at the time and I tried to explain the idea using a game. Imagine, I said, that we had to get to our destination three miles away without stopping. Almost at once the children could see the challenge. We couldn't predict what was going to happen in front of us and around us. We didn't know how long the light would stay on green or if the car in front would suddenly swerve or put on its brakes. The only way to keep from crashing was to put extra space between our car and the car in front of us. This space acted as a buffer. It gave us time to respond and adapt to any sudden or unexpected moves by other cars. It allowed us to avoid the friction of violent stops and starts.

Similarly, we can reduce the friction of executing the essential in our work and lives simply by creating a buffer.

During the car "game" with my children, they noticed that when I got distracted talking and laughing I would forget the buffer zone and get too close to the car in front of us. Then I would have to do something "unnatural" – like swerve or slam on the brakes at the last second – to adjust. A similar thing can happen if we forget to respect and maintain buffers in our lives. We get busy and distracted, and before we know it the project is due, the day of the big presentation has arrived – no matter how much extra time we built in. As a result we are forced to "swerve" or "slam on the brakes" at the last minute. From chemistry we know that gases expand to fill the space they are in; similarly, we've all experienced how projects and commitments tend to expand – despite our best efforts – to fill the amount of time allotted to them.

Just think of how often this happens in presentations, meetings, and workshops you have attended. How many times have you seen someone try to fit too many slides into too little time? How many times have you been to a conference where you felt that the presenter cut off a meaningful conversation because of feeling obliged to get through all the content he or she had planned? I have seen this so often, it has started to seem the default position. So when I worked with a facilitator who had a different philosophy it was truly liberating. He was designing a four-hour workshop. But instead of allowing the typical ten minutes at the end of the session for questions and comments he suggested a full hour. He explained, "I like to allow a luxurious amount of time just in case things come up." At first his idea was dismissed as indulgent, and he was instructed to go back to the traditional format. Sure enough, the class ran over its allotted time, and the facilitator had to try to rush through the remaining content. So the class was changed to allow the hour originally suggested. Things came up as he had expected, but this time there was a buffer built in. Now the class could end on time *and* the facilitator could focus on teaching, rather than rushing.

A mother I know learned a similar lesson when preparing to go on a holiday with her family. In the past, when they went on holiday she would leave the packing until the night before. Inevitably, she would end up staying up late, losing steam, getting too little sleep, finishing the packing in the morning, forgetting something, leaving late, and having to "push through" the long drive to compensate. This time, however, she started packing a week in advance. She made certain the car was fully packed the night before so that in the morning the only thing she had to do was wake up the children and get everyone in the car. It worked. They got off early, with a good night's sleep, nothing was forgotten, and when they hit traffic it wasn't stressful because they had a buffer for that possibility. As a result they not only arrived on time but enjoyed a frictionless and even pleasant journey.

The non-Essentialist tends to always assume a best-case scenario. We all know those people (and many of us, myself included, have been that person) who chronically underestimate how long something will really take: "This will just take five minutes," or "I'll be finished with that project by Friday," or "It will only take me a year to write my magnum opus." Yet inevitably these things take longer; something unexpected comes up, or the task ends up being more involved than anticipated, or the estimate was simply too optimistic in the first place. When this happens, they are left reacting to the problem, and results inevitably suffer. Perhaps they pull an all-nighter to make it happen. Perhaps they cut corners, hand in an incomplete project, or worse, fail to get it done at all. Or perhaps they leave someone else in the team to pick up the slack. Either way, they fail to execute at their highest level.

The way of the Essentialist is different. The Essentialist looks ahead. She plans. She prepares for different contingencies. She expects the unexpected. She creates a buffer to prepare for the unforeseen, thus giving herself some wiggle room when things come up, as they inevitably do.

Non-Essentialist	Essentialist
Assumes the best-case scenario will happen	Builds in a buffer for unexpected events
Forces execution at the last minute	Practises extreme and early preparation

When a non-Essentialist receives a windfall, she tends to consume it rather than to set it aside for a rainy day. We can see an example of this in the way nations have responded to finding oil. For example, in 1980, when Britain discovered North Sea oil, the government suddenly had a massive windfall in additional tax revenues, to the tune of £166 billion ($250 billion) over a decade.[1] Arguments can be made for and against how this money was used. But what is beyond dispute is that it was used; instead of creating an endowment to prepare against unexpected disasters (such as, in hindsight, the coming great recession), the British government spent it in other ways.

The way of the Essentialist, on the other hand, is to use the good times to create a buffer for the bad. Norway also benefited enormously from windfall taxes from oil but unlike Britain, Norway invested much of its good fortune in an endowment.[2] Today, this endowment has grown over time to be worth an extraordinary $720 billion, making it the world's largest sovereign wealth fund and providing a cushion against unknown future scenarios.[3]

These days the pace of our lives is only getting faster and faster. It is as if we are driving one inch behind another car at one hundred miles an hour. If that driver makes even the tiniest unexpected move – if he slows down even a little, or swerves even the smallest bit – we'll ram right into him. There is no room for error. As a result, execution is often highly stressful, frustrating, and forced.

Here are a few tips for keeping your work – and sanity – from swerving off the road by creating a buffer.

USE EXTREME PREPARATION

When I was a graduate student at Stanford I learned the key to receiving top grades was extreme preparation. The moment we received the syllabi for our classes I would make copies of them and paste together a calendar for the whole semester. Even before the first day of class I knew what the big projects were and would start on them immediately. This small investment in preparation reduced the stress of the entire semester because I knew I had plenty of time to get all the assignments done even if my workload suddenly got heavy, or if a family emergency forced me to miss some classes, or if any other unexpected event should happen.

The value of extreme preparation on a grander scale can be seen in the story of Roald Amundsen and Robert Falcon Scott in their race to be the first people in modern history to reach the South Pole. Both men had exactly the same objective. But their approaches differed.[4] Amundsen prepared for anything and everything that could possibly go wrong; Scott hoped for the best-case scenario. He brought just one thermometer for the trip and was furious when it broke. Amundsen brought four thermometers.

Scott stored one ton of food for his seventeen men. Amundsen stored three tons. Scott stashed supplies for the return journey in one spot marked with a single flag, meaning that if he went even a fraction off course his team could miss it. Amundsen, by contrast, planted twenty markers, miles apart, to ensure that his team would see them. Roald Amundsen prepared diligently and read obsessively for his journey, whereas Robert Falcon Scott did the bare minimum.

While Amundsen deliberately built slack and buffers into his plan, Scott hoped for the ideal circumstances. While Scott's men suffered from fatigue, hunger, and frostbite, Amundsen's team's journey was relatively (under the circumstances) frictionless. Amundsen successfully made the journey. Scott and his team tragically died.

The importance of extreme preparedness holds true for us in business. In fact, this example is used by Jim Collins and Morten Hansen to demonstrate why some companies have thrived under extreme and difficult circumstances while others have not. In filtering out 7 companies from 20,400, the authors found that the ones that executed most successfully did not have any better ability to predict the future than their less successful counterparts. Instead, they were the ones who acknowledged they could not predict the unexpected and therefore prepared better.[5]

ADD 50 PER CENT TO YOUR TIME ESTIMATE

I know someone who always thinks it will take her five minutes to get to the supermarket because she made the journey in five minutes *once*. The truth is it usually takes ten to fifteen minutes. In and of itself this would not be a huge problem, but unfortunately it is typical of most of her estimations in life. As a result she is perennially late and, to make matters worse, in a constant state of stress and guilt about it. She has been stuck in this cycle for so many years she no longer even recognises that she lives in constant stress. It has even affected her physically. But she still continues to believe she can make it to the supermarket in five minutes – or finish the conference call in half an hour or the major report in a week, or whatever else she is trying to squeeze in – and every once in a while she does. But the costs are high to her and the people around her. She would make a far greater contribution to all these rushed endeavours if she were simply to create a buffer.

Have you ever underestimated how long a task will take? If you have, you are far from alone. The term for this very common phenomenon is the "planning fallacy."[6] This term, coined by Daniel Kahneman in 1979, refers to people's tendency to underestimate how long a task will take, *even when they have actually done the task before*. In one study thirty-seven students were asked how long they thought it would take them to complete their thesis. When the students were asked to estimate how long it would take "if everything went as well as it possibly could," their averaged estimate was 27.4 days. When they were asked how long it would take "if everything went as poorly as it possibly could," their averaged estimate was 48.6 days. In the end the average time it actually took the students was 55.5 days. Only 30 per cent of the students completed the task in the time they had estimated.[7] Curiously, people will admit to having a tendency to underestimate while simultaneously believing their current estimates are accurate.[8]

Of the variety of explanations for why we underestimate the amount of time something will take, I believe social pressure is the most interesting. One study found that if people estimated *anonymously* how long it would take to complete a task they were no longer guilty of the planning fallacy.[9] This implies that often we actually *know* we can't do things in a given time frame, but we don't want to admit it to someone.

Whatever the reasons, the result is that we tend to be later than we say we will be: later to meetings, later to deliver things at work, later in paying our bills, and so on. Thus execution becomes frustrating when it could have been frictionless.

One way to protect against this is simply to add a 50 per cent buffer to the amount of time we estimate it will take to complete a task or project (if 50 per cent seems overly generous, consider how frequently things actually do take us 50 per cent longer than expected). So if you have an hour set aside for a conference call, block off an additional thirty minutes. If you've estimated it will take ten minutes to get your son to football practice, leave the house fifteen minutes before practice begins. Not only does this relieve the stress we feel about being late (imagine how much less stressful sitting in traffic would feel if we weren't running late), but if we do find that the task was faster and easier to execute than we expected (though this is a rare experience for most of us), the extra found time feels like a bonus.

CONDUCT SCENARIO PLANNING

Erwann Michel-Kerjan, the managing director of the Risk Management and Decision Processes Center at Wharton, University of Pennsylvania, recommends that everyone, starting with heads of state, develop a risk management strategy. For example, he has worked, in connection with the World Bank, to identify the most vulnerable countries in the world, and as a result Morocco, identified as number 58 out of the 85, has an action plan to prepare against areas of risk.[10]

When Erwann works with national governments to create their risk management strategies, he suggests they start by asking five questions: (1) What risks do we face and where? (2) What assets and populations are exposed and to what degree? (3) How vulnerable are they? (4) What financial burden do these risks place on individuals, businesses, and the government budget? and (5) How best can we invest to reduce risks and strengthen economic and social resilience?[11]

We can apply these five questions to our own attempts at building buffers. Think of the most important project you are trying to get done at work or at home. Then ask the following five questions: (1) What risks do you face on this project? (2) What is the worst-case scenario? (3) What would the social effects of this be? (4) What would the financial impact of this be? and (5) How can you invest to reduce risks or strengthen financial or social resilience? Your answer to that fifth and crucial question will point you to buffers – perhaps adding another 20 per cent to the project's budget, or getting a PR person on board to handle any potential negative press, or calling a board meeting to manage shareholder expectations – that you can create to safeguard you against unknowable events.

Essentialists accept the reality that we can never fully anticipate or prepare for every scenario or eventuality; the future is simply too unpredictable. Instead, they build in buffers to reduce the friction caused by the unexpected.

CHAPTER 16

SUBTRACT

Bring Forth More by Removing Obstacles

To attain knowledge add things every day. To
attain wisdom subtract things every day.

—*Lao-tzu*

In the business parable *The Goal,* Alex Rogo is a fictional character who is overwhelmed by the responsibility of turning around a failing production plant within three months.[1] At first he does not see how this is possible. Then he is mentored by a professor who tells him he can make incredible progress in a short time if only he can find the plant's "constraints." Constraints, he is told, are the obstacles holding the whole system back. Even if he improves everything else in the plant, his mentor tells him, if he doesn't address the constraints the plant will not materially improve.

As Alex is trying to make sense of what he is being taught, he goes on a hike with his son and some other friends. As the Scout leader, it's his responsibility to get all of the boys to the campsite before the sun sets. But as anyone who has been on such a hike knows, getting a group of young boys to keep up a pace is more difficult than it sounds, and Alex soon runs into a problem: some of the Scouts go really fast and others go really slow. One boy in particular, Herbie, is the slowest of all. The result is that the gap between the hikers at the front of the line and Herbie, the straggler, grows to be miles long.

At first Alex tries to manage the problem by getting the group at the front to stop and wait for the others to catch up. This keeps the group together for a time, but the moment they start walking again the same gap begins to form all over again.

So Alex decides to try a different approach. He puts Herbie at the *front* of the pack and lines up all the other boys in order of speed: slowest to fastest. It's counterintuitive to have the fastest person at the back of the line, but the moment he does it the pack begins to move in a single group. Every boy can keep up with the boy in front of him. The upside is that he can now keep an eye on the whole group at once, and they will all arrive at the campsite safely and at the same time. The downside is that the whole troop is now moving at Herbie's pace so they will arrive late. So what should he do?

The answer, Alex finds, is to do anything and everything to make things easier for Herbie. With the slowest boy at the front of the line, if Herbie moves one yard an hour faster, the whole troop will get there that much faster. That is an amazing insight to Alex. Any improvement with Herbie, however small, will improve the pace of the whole team immediately. So he actually takes weight out of Herbie's backpack (the extra food and supplies he brought with him) and distributes it throughout the rest of the group. And indeed, this instantly improves the speed of the whole group. They make it to camp in good time.

In a moment of insight, Alex sees how this approach could also be applied to turning around his production plant. Instead of trying to improve every aspect of the facility he needs to identify the "Herbie": the part of the process that is slower relative to every other part of the plant. He does this by finding which machine has the biggest queue of materials waiting behind it and finds a way to increase its efficiency. This in turn improves the next "slowest hiker's" efficiency, and so on, until the productivity of the whole plant begins to improve.

The question is this: What is the "slowest hiker" in your job or your life? What is the obstacle that is keeping you back from achieving what really matters to you? By systematically identifying and removing this "constraint" you'll be able to significantly reduce the friction keeping you from executing what is essential.

But this can't be done in a haphazard way. Simply finding things that need fixing here and there might lead to marginal, short-term improvements at best; at worst, you'll waste time and effort improving things that don't really matter. But if you really want to improve the overall functioning of the system – whether that system is a manufacturing process, a procedure in your department, or some routine in your daily life – you need to identify the "slowest hiker."

A non-Essentialist approaches execution in a reactive, haphazard manner. Because the non-Essentialist is always reacting to crises rather than anticipating them, he is forced to apply quick-fix solutions: the equivalent to plugging his finger into the hole of a leaking dam and hoping the whole thing doesn't burst. Being good with a hammer, the non-Essentialist thinks everything is a nail. Thus he applies more and more pressure, but this ends up only adding more friction and frustration. Indeed, in some situations the harder you push on someone the harder he or she will push back.

Essentialists don't default to Band-Aid solutions. Instead of looking for the most obvious or immediate obstacles, they look for the ones slowing down progress. They ask, "What is getting in the way of achieving what is essential?" While the non-Essentialist is busy applying more and more pressure and piling on more and more solutions, the Essentialist simply makes a one-time investment in removing obstacles. This approach goes beyond just solving problems; it's a method of reducing your efforts to maximise your results.

Non-Essentialist	Essentialist
Piles on quick-fix solutions	Removes obstacles to progress
Does more	Brings forth more

Produce More by Removing More

Aristotle talked about three kinds of work, whereas in our modern world we tend to emphasise only two. The first is theoretical work, for which the end goal is truth. The second is practical work, where the objective is action. But there is a third: it is *poietical* work.[2] The philosopher Martin Heidegger described poiesis as a "bringing-forth."[3] This third type of work is the Essentialist way of approaching execution:

An Essentialist produces more — brings forth more — by removing more instead of doing more.

Often we don't take the time to really think about which efforts will produce results and which will not. But even when we do, it is easier to think of execution in terms of addition rather than subtraction. If we want to sell more products, then we get more salespeople. If we want to produce more output, then we ramp up production. There is clearly evidence to support this approach. However, there is another way to think of improving results. Instead of focusing on the efforts and resources we need to add, the Essentialist focuses on the constraints or obstacles we need to remove. But how?

1. BE CLEAR ABOUT THE ESSENTIAL INTENT

We can't know what obstacles to remove until we are clear on the desired outcome. When we don't know what we're really trying to achieve, all change is arbitrary. So ask yourself, "How will we know when we are done?" For the purposes of this chapter, let's say your goal is to get a draft of a fifteen-page, written report attached to an e-mail and sent to the client by 2 p.m. on Thursday. Note: this is deliberately a precise outcome, not a vague one.

2. IDENTIFY THE "SLOWEST HIKER"

Instead of just jumping into the project, take a few minutes to think. Ask yourself, "What are all the obstacles standing between me and getting this done?" and "What is keeping me from completing this?" Make a list of these obstacles. They might include: not having the information you need, your energy level, your desire for perfection. Prioritise the list using the question, "What is the obstacle that, if removed, would make the majority of other obstacles disappear?"

When identifying your "slowest hiker," one important thing to keep in mind is that even activities that are "productive" – like doing research, or e-mailing people for information, or rewriting the report in order to get it perfect the first time around – can be obstacles. Remember, the desired goal is to get a draft of the report finished. Anything slowing down the execution of that goal should be questioned.

There are often multiple obstacles to achieving any essential intent. However, at any one time there is only ever one priority; removing arbitrary obstacles can have no effect whatsoever if the primary one still doesn't budge. To take our example, if getting words on the page is your primary obstacle, you could hire someone to do research for you and still be no closer to writing the aforementioned report. So just as Alex fixes the least efficient machine first, followed by the second least efficient, and so on – instead of trying to fix them all at once – we too must tackle the removal of obstacles one by one.

3. REMOVE THE OBSTACLE

Let's say your "slowest hiker" turns out to be your desire to make the report perfect. There may be dozens of ideas you have to make the report better, but in this case your essential intent is to send off the draft. So to remove the obstacle you need to replace the idea "This has to be perfect or else" with "Done is better than perfect." Give yourself permission not to have it polished in the first draft. By removing the primary obstacle you have made every other aspect of the job easier.

The "slowest hiker" could even be another person – whether it's a boss who won't give the green light on a project, the finance department who won't approve the budget, or a client who won't sign on the dotted line. To reduce the friction with another person, apply the "catch more flies with honey" approach. Send him an e-mail, but instead of asking if he has done the work for you (which obviously he hasn't), go and see him. Ask him, "What obstacles or bottlenecks are holding you back from achieving X, and how can I help remove these?" Instead of pestering him, offer sincerely to support him. You will get a warmer reply than you would by just e-mailing him another demand.

When our children were really little and I was a postgraduate student, my wife was feeling strained by the demands of looking after the children all day every day, and didn't know quite what to do about it. I was reading about the Theory of Constraints at the time so it was particularly on my mind. As we applied the steps above, we realised the primary obstacle keeping her from making her highest point of contribution in our children's lives was a lack of time to plan, think, and prepare; after all, with three little children it was nearly impossible to have uninterrupted time. So we worked to remove this obstacle. I opted out of many of the extracurricular activities to be home in the evenings and we found someone who would look after the children for a few hours during the week. As a result, we were able to be more fully engaged and present during the time we spent with our children. In other words, we both actually ended up doing less, but better.

Removing obstacles does not have to be hard or take a superhuman effort. Instead, we can start small. It's kind of like dislodging a boulder at the top of a hill. All it takes is a small shove, then momentum will naturally build.

CHAPTER 17

PROGRESS

The Power of Small Wins

EVERY DAY DO SOMETHING THAT WILL INCH YOU
CLOSER TO A BETTER TOMORROW.

—Doug Firebaugh

Think of the last time you were pulled over by the police while driving. Did you wonder to yourself: "Is this going to be a good ticket or a bad one?" Not likely. Everyone knows tickets are all bad, right? Yet at least one innovative police department in Richmond, Canada, thinks this is an assumption that ought to be challenged.[1]

There is a well-established approach to cracking down on crime: pass new and harsher laws, set stronger sentencing, or initiate zero-tolerance initiatives. In other words, do more of what we already do – only more forcefully. For years, the Richmond Police Department followed these core and long-held practices of policing systems everywhere and experienced the typical results: recidivism rates at 65 per cent and spiralling youth crime. That is, until a young, forward-thinking new superintendent, Ward Clapham, came in and challenged them.[2] Why, he asked, do all of our policing efforts have to be so reactive, so negative, and so after the fact? What if, instead of just focusing on catching criminals – and serving up ever harsher punishments – *after* they committed the crime, the police devoted significant resources and effort to eliminating criminal behaviour *before* it happens? To quote Tony Blair, what if they could be tough on crime but also tough on the *causes* of crime?[3]

Out of these questions came the novel idea for Positive Tickets, a programme whereby police, instead of focusing on catching young people perpetrating crimes, would focus on catching youth doing something *good* – something as simple as throwing litter away in a bin rather than on the ground, wearing a helmet while riding their bike, skateboarding in the designated area, or getting to school on time – and would give them a ticket for *positive* behaviour. The ticket, of course, wouldn't carry a fine like a parking ticket but instead would be redeemable for some kind of small reward, like free entry to the movies or to an event at a local youth centre – wholesome activities that also had the bonus of keeping the young people off the streets and out of trouble.

So how well did Richmond's unconventional effort to reimagine policing work? Amazingly well, as it turned out. It took some time, but they invested in the approach as a long-term strategy, and after a decade the Positive Tickets system had reduced recidivism from 60 per cent to 8 per cent.

You might not think of a police department as a place where you would expect to see Essentialism at work, but in fact Ward's system of Positive Tickets is a lesson in the practice of effortless execution.

The way of the non-Essentialist is to go big on everything: to try to do it all, have it all, fit it all in. The non-Essentialist operates under the false logic that the more he strives, the more he will achieve, but the reality is, the more we reach for the stars, the harder it is to get ourselves off the ground.

The way of the Essentialist is different. Instead of trying to accomplish it all – and all at once – and flaring out, the Essentialist starts small and celebrates progress. Instead of going for the big, flashy wins that don't really matter, the Essentialist pursues small and simple wins in areas that are essential.

Non-Essentialist	Essentialist
Starts with a big goal and gets small results	Starts small and gets big results
Goes for the flashiest wins	Celebrates small acts of progress

By catching and rewarding people in the midst of "small wins," Ward Clapham's approach tapped into the power of celebrating progress. In one moving example, a police officer pulled over a teenager who had saved a girl from being hit by a car, gave him a Positive Ticket, and said: "You did a great thing today. You can make a difference." The boy went home and put the Positive Ticket on his wall. After a few weeks his foster mother asked him whether he was going to cash it in. To her surprise he said he never would. An adult had told him he could be somebody, and that was worth more than free pizza or bowling.

Multiply that type of positive interaction by forty thousand times a year for ten years and you can sense why it started to make a difference. Each time a young person was recognised and commended for doing something good, he or she was that much more motivated to continue doing good until, eventually, doing good became natural and effortless.

When we want to create major change we often think we need to lead with something huge or grandiose, like the executive I knew who announced with great fanfare that he had decided to build his daughters an elaborate dolls house – but then, because his visions for it were so large and ambitious, abandoned the project as too burdensome. There is an appealing logic to this: that to do something big we have to start big. However, just think of all of the "big," hyped-up initiatives in organisations that never ended up amounting to anything – just like that executive's dolls house.

Research has shown that of all forms of human motivation the most effective one is progress. Why? Because a small, concrete win creates momentum and affirms our faith in our further success. In his 1968 *Harvard Business Review* article entitled "One More Time: How Do You Motivate Employees?" among the most popular *Harvard Business Review* articles of all time, Frederick Herzberg reveals research showing that the two primary internal motivators for people are achievement and recognition for achievement.[4] More recently, Teresa Amabile and Steven Kramer gathered anonymous diary entries from hundreds of people and covering thousands of workdays. On the basis of these hundreds of thousands of reflections, Amabile and Kramer concluded that "everyday progress – even a small win" can make all the difference in how people feel and perform. "Of all the things that can boost emotions, motivation, and perceptions during a workday, the single most important is making progress in meaningful work," they said.[5]

Instead of starting big and then flaring out with nothing to show for it other than time and energy wasted, to really get essential things done we need to start small and build momentum. Then we can use that momentum to work towards the next win, and the next one and so on until we have a significant breakthrough – and when we do, our progress will have become so frictionless and effortless that the breakthrough will seem like overnight success. As former Stanford professor and educator Henry B. Eyring has written, "My experience has taught me this about how people and organizations improve: the best place to look is for small changes we could make in the things we do often. There is power in steadiness and repetition."[6]

When I met Dr Phil Zimbardo, the former president of the American Psychological Association, for lunch, I knew him primarily as the mastermind behind the famous Stanford prison experiment.[7] In the summer of 1971, Zimbardo took healthy Stanford students, assigned them roles as either "guards" or "inmates," and locked them in a makeshift "prison" in the basement of Stanford University. In just days, the "prisoners" began to demonstrate symptoms of depression and extreme stress, while the "guards" began to act cruel and sadistic (the experiment was ended early, for obvious reasons). The point is that simply being *treated like* prisoners and guards had, over the course of just a few days, created a momentum that caused the subjects to *act like* prisoners and guards.

The Stanford prison experiment is legendary, and much has been written about its many implications. But what I wondered was this: If simply being treated in a certain way conditioned these Stanford students gradually to adopt these negative behaviours, could the same kind of conditioning work for more positive behaviour too?

Indeed, today Zimbardo is attempting a grand social experiment along those lines called the "Heroic Imagination Project."[8] The logic is to increase the odds of people operating with courage by teaching them the principles of heroism. By encouraging and rewarding heroic acts, Zimbardo believes, we can consciously and deliberately create a system where heroic acts eventually become natural and effortless.

We have a choice. We can use our energies to set up a system that makes execution of goodness easy, or we can resign ourselves to a system that actually makes it harder to do what is good. Ward's Positive Tickets system did the former, and it worked. We can apply the same principle to the choices we face when designing systems in our own lives.

My wife Anna and I have tried to apply these ideas to our system of parenting. At one point, we had become concerned with how much screen time had crept into our family. Between television, computers, tablets, and smartphones it had become just too easy for the children to waste time on non-essential entertainment. But our attempts to get them to change these habits, as you can imagine, were met with friction. The children would complain whenever we turned the TV off or tried to limit their "screen time." And we as the parents had to consciously police the situation, which took *us* away from doing things that were essential.

So we introduced a token system.[9] The children were given ten tokens at the beginning of the week. These could each be traded in for either thirty minutes of screen time or fifty cents at the end of the week, adding up to $5 or five hours of screen time a week. If a child read a book for thirty minutes, he or she would earn an additional token, which could also be traded in for screen time or for money. The results were incredible: overnight, screen time went down 90 per cent, reading went up by the same amount, *and* the overall effort we had to put into policing the system went way, way down. In other words, non-essential activity dramatically decreased and essential activity dramatically increased. Once a small amount of initial effort was invested to set up the system, it worked without friction.

We can all create systems like this both at home and at work. The key is to start small, encourage progress, and celebrate small wins. Here are a few techniques.

FOCUS ON MINIMAL VIABLE PROGRESS

A popular idea in Silicon Valley is "Done is better than perfect."[10] The sentiment is not that we should produce rubbish. The idea, as I read it, is not to waste time on non-essentials and just to get the thing done. In entrepreneurial circles the idea is expressed as creating a "minimal viable product."[11] The idea is, "What is the simplest possible product that will be useful and valuable to the intended customer?"

Similarly, we can adopt a method of "minimal viable progress." We can ask ourselves, "What is the smallest amount of progress that will be useful and valuable to the essential task we are trying to get done?" I used this practice in writing this book. For example, when I was still in the exploratory mode of the book, before I'd even begun to put pen to paper (or fingers to keyboard), I would share a short idea (my minimal viable product) on Twitter. If it seemed to resonate with people there, I would write a blog piece on *Harvard Business Review*. Through this iterative process, which required very little effort, I was able to find where there seemed to be a connection between what I was thinking and what seemed to have the highest relevancy in other people's lives.

It is the process Pixar uses in their movies. Instead of starting with a script, they start with storyboards – or what have been described as the comic book version of a movie. They try ideas out and see what works. They do this in small cycles hundreds of times. Then they put out a movie to small groups of people to give them advance feedback. This allows them to learn as quickly as possible with as little effort as possible. As John Lasseter, the chief creative officer at Pixar and now Disney, said, "We don't actually finish our films, we release them."[12]

DO THE MINIMAL VIABLE PREPARATION

There are two opposing ways to approach an important goal or deadline. You can start early and small or start late and big. "Late and big" means doing it all at the last minute: pulling an all-nighter and "making it happen." "Early and small" means starting at the earliest possible moment with the minimal possible time investment.

Often just ten minutes invested in a project or assignment two weeks before it is due can save you much frantic and stressed-out scrambling at the eleventh hour. Take a goal or deadline you have coming up and ask yourself, "What is the minimal amount I could do *right now* to prepare?"

One leader who is an exceptionally inspiring speaker has explained that the key for him is to start to prepare his big speeches six months before he does them. He isn't preparing the entire speech; he just starts. If you have a big presentation coming up over the next few weeks or months, open a file right now and spend four minutes starting to put down any ideas. Then close the file. No more than four minutes. Just start it.

A colleague in New York uses a simple tactic: whenever she schedules a meeting or phone call, she takes exactly fifteen seconds to type up the main objectives for that meeting, so on the morning of the meeting when she sits down to prepare talking points she can refer to them. She doesn't need to plan the whole meeting agenda. Just a few seconds of early preparation pay a valuable dividend.

VISUALLY REWARD PROGRESS

Do you remember when you were five years old and your school held a fund-raiser? Remember the big thermometer that visually showed the progress the school was making towards the goal? Can you remember how exciting and motivating it was to watch the level of the thermometer go up each day? Or perhaps your parents had a star chart for you. Every time you ate your spinach, or went to bed on time, or cleaned your room you got a star, and pretty soon you were doing those things virtually without any prodding.

There is something powerful about visibly seeing progress towards a goal. Don't be above applying the same technique to your own essential goals, at home or at work.

When we start small and reward progress, we end up achieving *more* than when we set big, lofty, and often impossible goals. And as a bonus, the act of positively reinforcing our successes allows us to reap more enjoyment and satisfaction out of the process.

CHAPTER 18

FLOW

The Genius of Routine

ROUTINE, IN AN INTELLIGENT MAN,
IS A SIGN OF AMBITION.

—*W. H. Auden*

For years before the Olympic swimmer Michael Phelps won the gold at the 2008 Beijing Olympics, he followed the same routine at every race. He arrived two hours early.[1] He stretched and loosened up, according to a precise pattern: eight hundred mixer, fifty freestyle, six hundred kicking with kickboard, four hundred pulling a buoy, and more. After the warm-up he would dry off, put in his earphones, and sit – never lie down – on the massage table. From that moment, he and his coach, Bob Bowman, wouldn't speak a word to each other until after the race was over.

At forty-five minutes before the race he would put on his race suit. At thirty minutes he would get into the warm-up pool and do six hundred to eight hundred metres. With ten minutes to go he would walk to the "ready room". He would find a seat alone, never next to anyone. He liked to keep the seats on both sides of him clear for his things: goggles on one side and his towel on the other. When his race was called he would walk to the blocks. There he would do what he always did: two stretches, first a straight-leg stretch and then with a bent knee. Left leg first every time. Then the right earbud would come out. When his name was called, he would take out the left earbud. He would step onto the block – always from the left side. He would dry the block – every time. Then he would stand and flap his arms in such a way that his hands hit his back.

Phelps explained: "It's just a routine. My routine. It's the routine I've gone through my whole life. I'm not going to change it." And that is that. His coach, Bob Bowman, designed this physical routine with Phelps. But that's not all. He also gave Phelps a routine for what to think about as he went to sleep and first thing when he awoke. He called it "Watching the Videotape."[2] There was no actual tape, of course. The "tape" was a visualisation of the perfect race. In exquisite detail and slow motion Phelps would visualise every moment from his starting position on top of the blocks, through each stroke, until he emerged from the pool, victorious, with water dripping off his face.

Phelps didn't do this mental routine occasionally. He did it every day before he went to bed and every day when he woke up – for years. When Bob wanted to challenge him in practices he would shout, "Put in the videotape!" and Phelps would push beyond his limits. Eventually the mental routine was so deeply ingrained that Bob barely had to whisper the phrase, "Get the videotape ready," before a race. Phelps was always ready to "hit play."

When asked about the routine, Bowman said: "If you were to ask Michael what's going on in his head before competition, he would say he's not really thinking about anything. He's just following the program. But that's not right. It's more like his habits have taken over. When the race arrives, he's more than halfway through his plan and he's been victorious at every step. All the stretches went like he planned. The warm-up laps were just like he visualised.

His headphones are playing exactly what he expected. The actual race is just another step in a pattern that started earlier that day and has been nothing but victories. Winning is a natural extension."[3]

As we all know, Phelps won the record eight gold medals at the 2008 Beijing Olympics. When visiting Beijing, years after Phelps's breathtaking accomplishment, I couldn't help but think about how Phelps and the other Olympians make all these feats of amazing athleticism seem so effortless. Of course Olympic athletes arguably practise longer and train harder than any other athletes in the world – but when they get in that pool, or on that track, or onto that rink, they make it look positively easy. It's more than just a natural extension of their training. It's a testament to the genius of the right routine.

The way of the non-Essentialist is to think the essentials only get done when they are forced. That execution is a matter of raw effort alone. You labour to make it happen. You push through.

The way of the Essentialist is different. The Essentialist designs a routine that makes achieving what you have identified as essential to the default position. Yes, in some instances an Essentialist still has to work hard, but with the right routine in place each effort yields exponentially greater results.

Non-Essentialist	Essentialist
Tries to execute the essentials by force	Designs a routine that enshrines what is essential, making execution almost effortless
Allows non-essentials to be the default	Makes the essential the default position

Making It Look Easy

Routine is one of the most powerful tools for removing obstacles. Without routine, the pull of non-essential distractions will overpower us. But if we create a routine that enshrines the essentials, we will begin to execute them on autopilot. Instead of our consciously pursuing the essential, it will happen without our having to think about it. We won't have to expend precious energy every day prioritising everything. We must simply expend a small amount of initial energy to create the routine, and then all that is left to do is follow it.

There is a huge body of scientific research to explain the mechanism by which routine enables difficult things to become easy. One simplified explanation is that as we repeatedly do a certain task the neurons, or nerve cells, make new connections through communication gateways called "synapses." With repetition, the connections strengthen and it becomes easier for the brain to activate them. For example, when you learn a new word it takes several repetitions at various intervals for the word to be mastered. To recall the word later you will need to activate the same synapses until eventually you know the word without consciously thinking about it.[4]

A similar process explains how when we drive from point A to point B every day we can eventually make the journey without consciously thinking about it, or why once we've cooked the same meal a few times we no longer have to consult the recipe, or why any mental task gets easier and easier each time we attempt it. With repetition the routine is mastered and the activity becomes second nature.

Our ability to execute the essential improves with practice, just like any other ability. Think about the first time you had to perform a certain critical function at work. At first you felt like a novice. You probably felt unsure and awkward. The effort to focus drained your willpower. Decision fatigue set in. You were probably easily distracted. This is perfectly normal. But once you performed the function over and over again, you gained confidence. You were no longer sidetracked. You were able to perform the function better and faster, and with less concentration and effort. This power of a routine grows out of our brain's ability to take over entirely until the process becomes fully unconscious.

There is another cognitive advantage to routine as well. Once the mental work shifts to the basal ganglia, mental space is freed up to concentrate on something new. This allows us to autopilot the execution of one essential activity while simultaneously actively engaging in another, without sacrificing our level of focus or contribution. "In fact, the brain starts working less and less," says Charles Duhigg, author of the book *The Power of Habit*. "The brain can almost completely shut down. . . . And this is a real advantage, because it means you have all of this mental activity you can devote to something else."[5]

To some, routine can sound like where creativity and innovation go to die – the ultimate exercise in boredom. We even use the word as a synonym for *pallid* and *bland,* as in "It has just become *routine* for me." And routines can indeed become this – the wrong routines. But the right routines can actually enhance innovation and creativity by giving us the equivalent of an energy rebate. Instead of spending our limited supply of discipline on making the same decisions again and again, embedding our decisions into our routine allows us to channel that discipline towards some other essential activity.

The work Mihaly Csikszentmihalyi has done on creativity demonstrates how highly creative people use strict routines to free up their minds. "Most creative individuals find out early what their best rhythms are for sleeping, eating, and working, and abide by them even when it is tempting to do otherwise," Mihaly says. "They wear clothes that are comfortable, they interact only with people they find congenial, they do only things they think are important. Of course, such idiosyncrasies are not endearing to those they have to deal with. . . . But personalizing patterns of action helps to free the mind from the expectations that make demands on attention and allows intense concentration on matters that count."[6]

One CEO in one of Silicon Valley's most innovative companies has what at first glance would seem like a boring, creativity-killing routine. He holds a three-hour meeting that starts at 9 a.m. one day a week. It is *never* missed. It is never rescheduled at a different time. It is mandatory – so much so that even in this global firm all the executives know never to schedule any travel that will conflict with the meeting. If it is 9 a.m. on Monday, every person will be there. It is a discipline. At first blush there is nothing particularly unique about this. But what *is* unique is the quality of ideas that come out of this regular meeting. Because the CEO has eliminated the mental cost involved in planning the meeting or thinking about who will or won't be there, people can focus on the creative problem solving. And indeed, his team makes coming up with creative, inventive ideas and solutions look natural and easy.

The Power of the *Right* Routine

According to researchers at Duke University in North Carolina, nearly 40 per cent of our choices are deeply unconscious.[7] We don't think about them in the usual sense. There is both danger and opportunity in this. The opportunity is that we can develop new abilities that eventually become instinctive. The danger is that we may develop routines that are counterproductive. Without being fully aware, we can get caught in non-essential habits – like checking our e-mail the second we get out of bed every morning, or picking up a doughnut on the way home from work each day, or spending our lunch hour trolling the Internet instead of using the time to think, reflect, recharge, or connect with friends and colleagues. So how can we discard the routines that keep us locked in non-essential habits and replace them with routines that make executing essentials almost effortless?

OVERHAUL YOUR TRIGGERS

Most of us have a behavioural habit we want to change, whether it's to eat less junk food, waste less time, or worry less. But when we try, we find that changing even the simplest, tiniest habit is amazingly, disturbingly hard. There seems to be a gravitational force pulling us inexorably back to the warm embrace of those French fries, that Web site with the pictures of the goofy cats, or the spiral of worry about things outside our control. How do we resist the powerful pull of these habits?

In an interview about his book *The Power of Habit* Charles Duhigg said "in the last 15 years, as we've learned how habits work and how they can be changed, scientists have explained that every habit is made up of a cue, a routine, and a reward. The cue is a trigger that tells your brain to go into automatic mode and which habit to use. Then there is the routine – the behaviour itself – which can be physical or mental or emotional. Finally, there is a reward, which helps your brain figure out if this particular habit is worth remembering for the future. Over time, this loop – cue, routine, reward; cue, routine, reward – becomes more automatic as the cue and reward become neurologically intertwined."[8]

What this means is that if we want to change our routine, we don't really need to change the behaviour. Rather, we need to find the *cue* that is triggering the non-essential activity or behaviour and find a way to associate that same cue with something that *is* essential. So, for example, if the bakery you pass on the way home from work triggers you to pick up a doughnut, next time you pass by that bakery, use that cue to remind you to pick up a salad from the deli across the street. Or if your alarm clock going off in the morning triggers you to check your e-mail, use it as a cue to get up and read instead. At first, overcoming the temptation to stop at the bakery or check the e-mail will be difficult. But each time you execute the new behaviour – each time you pick up the salad – strengthens the link in your brain between the cue and the new behaviour, and soon, you'll be *subconsciously and automatically* performing the new routine.

CREATE NEW TRIGGERS

If the goal is to create some behavioural change, we're not just confined to our existing cues; we can create brand-new ones to trigger the execution of some essential routine. I used this technique to develop the daily routine of writing in a journal, and it worked wonders for me. For a long time I wrote in my journal only sporadically. I would put it off all day; then at night I would rationalise, "I will do it in the morning." But inevitably I wouldn't, and then by the next night I had two days' worth to write and it was overwhelming. So I put it off again. And so on. Then I heard someone say he had developed a routine of writing a few lines at the exact same time each day. This seemed like a manageable habit, but I knew that I would need some cue reminding me to write at the specified time each day or I would continue to put it off as I'd been doing. So I started putting my journal in my bag right next to my phone. That way, when I pull my phone out of my bag to charge it each evening (already a well-established habit) I see the journal, and this cues me to write in it. Now it is instinctive. Natural. I look forward to it. It has been ten years now and I have almost never missed a day.

DO THE MOST DIFFICULT THING FIRST

Ray Zinn is the founder and CEO of Micrel, a semiconductor business in Silicon Valley. He is a contrarian in lots of ways. He is seventy-five years old in an industry and city that usually celebrates twenty-year-old college dropouts. In 1978 he and his business partner invested $300,000 to launch the company and it has been profitable every single year, since inception (except for one year when they consolidated two manufacturing facilities). Since going public, their stock price has never fallen below its launch price. Ray credits this success to their highly disciplined focus on profitability. He has led the company as CEO for thirty-five years, and throughout that period Ray has followed an extraordinarily consistent routine. He wakes up at 5:30 a.m. every single morning, including Saturday and Sunday (as he's done for more than fifty years). He then exercises for an hour. He eats breakfast at 7:30 a.m. and arrives at work at 8:15 a.m. Dinner is at 6:30 p.m. with his family. Bedtime is 10 p.m. But what really enables Ray to operate at his highest level of contribution is that throughout the day, his routine is governed by a single rule: "Focus on the hardest thing first." After all, as Ray said to me: "We already have too much to think about. Why not eliminate some of them by establishing a routine?"

Use the tips above to develop a routine of doing your hardest task of the day first thing in the morning. Find a cue – whether it's that first glass of orange juice you have at your desk, or an alarm you set on your mobile phone, or anything you're already accustomed to doing first thing in the morning – to trigger you to sit down and focus on your hardest thing.

MIX UP YOUR ROUTINES

It's true that doing the same things at the same time, day after day, can get boring. To avoid this kind of routine fatigue, there's no reason why you can't have different routines for different days of the week. Jack Dorsey, the co-founder of Twitter and founder of Square, has an interesting approach to his weekly routine. He has divided up his week into themes. Monday is for management meetings and "running the company" work. Tuesday is for product development. Wednesday is for marketing, communications, and growth. Thursday is for developers and partnerships. Friday is for the company and its culture.[9] This routine helps to provide calmness amid the chaos of a high-growth start-up. It enables him to focus his energy on a single theme each day instead of feeling pulled into everything. He adheres to this routine each week, no exceptions, and over time people learn this about him and can organise meetings and requests around it.

TACKLE YOUR ROUTINES ONE BY ONE

It would be unfortunate to become so taken with the genius of routine that we'd be tempted to try to overhaul multiple routines at the same time. But as we learned in the last chapter, to get big results we must start small. So start with one change in your daily or weekly routine and then build on your progress from there.

I don't want to imply that any of this is easy. Many of our non-essential routines are deep and emotional. They have been formed in the furnace of some strong emotions. The idea that we can just snap our fingers and replace them with a new one is naive. Learning essential new skills is never easy. But once we master them and make them automatic we have won an enormous victory, because the skill remains with us for the rest of our lives. The same is true with routines. Once they are in place they are gifts that keep on giving.

CHAPTER 19

FOCUS

What's Important Now?

LIFE IS AVAILABLE ONLY IN THE PRESENT MOMENT.
IF YOU ABANDON THE PRESENT MOMENT YOU CANNOT
LIVE THE MOMENTS OF YOUR DAILY LIFE DEEPLY.
—*Thich Nhat Hanh*

Larry Gelwix coached the Highland High School, Salt Lake City, rugby team to 418 wins with only ten losses and twenty national championships over thirty-six years. He describes his success this way: "We always win." With a record like Highland's he has the right to make the statement. But he is actually referring to something more than his winning record. When he says, "win," he's also referring to a single question, with its apt acronym, that guides what he expects from his players: "What's important now?"

By keeping his players fully present in the moment and fully focused on what is most important – not on next week's match, or tomorrow's practice, or the next play, but *now* – Gelwix helps make winning almost effortless. But how?

First, the players apply the question constantly throughout the game. Instead of getting caught up rehashing the last play that went wrong, or spending their mental energy worrying about whether they are going to lose the game, neither of which is helpful or constructive, Larry encourages them to focus only on the play they are in *right now*.

Second, the question "What's important now?" helps them stay focused on how *they are playing*. Larry believes a huge part of winning is determined by whether the players are focused on their own game or on their opponent's game. If the players start thinking about the other team they lose focus. Consciously or not, they start wanting to play the way the other team is playing. They get distracted and divided. By focusing on *their* game in the here and now, they can all unite around a single strategy. This level of unity makes execution of their game plan relatively frictionless.

Indeed, Larry has a fundamentally Essentialist approach to winning and losing. As he tells his players: "There is a difference between losing and being beaten. Being beaten means they are better than you. They are faster, stronger, and more talented." To Larry, losing means something else. It means you lost focus. It means you didn't concentrate on what was essential. It is all based on a simple but powerful idea: to operate at your highest level of contribution requires that you deliberately tune in to what is important in the here and now.

There Is Only Now

Think about how this might apply in your own life. Have you ever become trapped reliving past mistakes ... over and over like a video player, stuck on endless replay? Do you spend time and energy worrying about the future? Do you spend more time thinking about the things you can't control rather than the things you can control about the areas where your efforts matter? Do you ever find yourself busy trying to prepare mentally for the next meeting, or the next assignment, or the next chapter in your life, rather than being fully present in the current one? It's natural and human to obsess over past mistakes or feel stress about what may be ahead of us. Yet every second spent worrying about a past or future moment distracts us from what is important in the here and now.

The ancient Greeks had two words for time. The first was *chronos*. The second was *kairos*. The Greek god Chronos was imagined as an elderly, grey-haired man, and his name connotes the literal ticking clock, the chronological time, the kind we measure (and race about trying to use efficiently). *Kairos* is different. While it is difficult to translate precisely, it refers to time that is opportune, right, different. *Chronos* is quantitative; *kairos* is qualitative. The latter is experienced only when we are fully in the moment – when we exist in the *now*.

It is mind-bending to consider that in practical terms we only ever have now. We can't control the future in a literal sense, just the now. Of course, we learn from the past and can imagine the future. Yet only in the here and now can we actually execute on the things that really matter.

Non-Essentialists tend to be so preoccupied with past successes and failures, as well as future challenges and opportunities, that they miss the present moment. They become distracted. Unfocused. They aren't really there.

The way of the Essentialist is to tune into the present. To experience life in *kairos*, not just *chronos*. To focus on the things that are truly important – not yesterday or tomorrow, but right now.

Non-Essentialist	Essentialist
Mind is spinning out about the past or the future	Mind is focused on the present
Thinks about what was important yesterday or tomorrow	Tunes in to what is important right now
Worries about the future or stresses about the past	Enjoys the moment

Recently Anna and I met for lunch in the middle of a busy workday. Usually when we meet for lunch we're so busy catching each other up on the events of our mornings or planning the activities for the evening that we forget to enjoy the act of having lunch together in the here and now. So this time, as the food arrived, Anna suggested an experiment: we should focus only on the moment. No rehashing our morning meetings, no talking about who would pick up the children from karate or what we'd cook for dinner that night. We should eat slowly and deliberately, fully focused on the present. I was totally game for it.

As I slowly took my first bite something happened. I noticed my breathing. Then without conscious intent I found it slowing. Suddenly, time itself felt as if it was moving slower. Instead of feeling as if my body was in one place and my mind was in five other places, I felt as though both my mind and my body were fully there.

The sensation stayed with me into the afternoon, where I noticed another change. Instead of being interrupted by distracting thoughts, I was able to give my full concentration to my work. Because I was calm and present on the tasks at hand, each one flowed naturally. Instead of my usual state of having my mental energies split and scattered across many competing subjects, my state was one of being focused on the subject that was most important in the present. Getting my work done not only became more effortless but actually gave me joy. In this case, what was good for the mind was also good for the soul.

Jiro Ono is the world's greatest sushi chef and the subject of the movie *Jiro Dreams of Sushi,* directed by David Geld.[1] At eighty-five years of age, he has been making sushi for decades, and indeed for him the art of making sushi has become nearly effortless. Yet his isn't simply the story of how practice and experience lead to mastery. Watching him work, you see someone entirely in the moment.

Essentialists live their whole lives in this manner. And because they do, they can apply their full energy to the job at hand. They don't diffuse their efforts with distractions. They know that execution is easy if you work hard at it and hard if you work easy at it.

Multi-tasking Versus Multi-focusing

I ran into a former classmate of mine years after graduating from Stanford. I was on campus doing some work on a computer in one of the offices when he came over to me to say hi. After a minute of pleasantries he told me he was in between jobs. He explained a little about the job he was looking for and asked if I could help him. I started asking him some questions to see how I could be helpful to him, but twenty seconds into the conversation he got a text on his phone. Without saying a word, he looked down and started responding to it. I did what I typically do when that happens. I paused and waited.

Ten seconds went by. Then twenty. I simply stood there as he continued to text away furiously. He didn't say anything. He didn't acknowledge me. Out of curiosity I waited to see how long it would go on. But after two full minutes, which is quite a lot of time when you are standing waiting for someone, I gave up, walked back to my desk, and went back to my work. After another five minutes he became present again, interrupting me for the second time. Now he wanted to resume the conversation, to ask for help with his job search again. Initially I had been ready to recommend him for a job opening I knew of, but after this incident I admit to feeling hesitant about recommending him for an interview where he might suddenly not be present: he'd be present in body, perhaps, but not in mind.

At this point you might expect me to start talking about the evils of multi-tasking – about how a true Essentialist never attempts to do more than one thing at a time. But in fact we can easily do two things at the same time: wash the dishes and listen to the radio, eat and talk, clear the clutter on our desk while thinking about where to go for lunch, text message while watching television, and so on.

What we can't do is *concentrate* on two things at the same time. When I talk about being present, I'm not talking about doing only one thing at a time. I'm talking about being focused on one thing at a time. Multi-tasking itself is not the enemy of Essentialism; pretending we can "multi-*focus*" is.

How to Be in the Now

What can we do to be fully present in what is in front of us? Below are some simple techniques to consider.

FIGURE OUT WHAT IS MOST IMPORTANT RIGHT NOW

Recently I had taught a full day on Essentialism to an executive team in New York. I had thoroughly enjoyed the day and had felt present throughout. But by the time I returned to my room I felt a sudden pull in a million directions. Everything around me was a reminder of all of the things I could be doing: check my e-mail, listen to messages, read a book I felt obliged to read, prepare the presentation for a few weeks from now, record interesting ideas that had grown out of the day's experiences, and more. It wasn't just the sheer number of things that felt overwhelming, it was that familiar stress of many tasks vying for top billing at the same time. As I felt the anxiety and tension rise I stopped. I knelt down. I closed my eyes and asked, "What's important *now*?" After a moment of reflection I realised that until I knew what was important right now, what was important right now was to figure out what was important right now!

I stood up. I tidied up. I put all of the objects strewn around me away, in their proper place, so they wouldn't distract me and pressure me to do their bidding every time I walked by. I turned off my phone. It was such a relief to have a barrier between me and someone's ability to text me. I opened my journal and wrote about the day. It centred me. I wrote a list in pencil of all the things on my mind. Then I clarified this by asking, "What do you need to do to be able to go to sleep peacefully?" What was essential, I decided, was to connect with my wife and children. Then it was to do just those few things that would make the first few hours of the next morning as effortless as possible: schedule a wake-up call and breakfast in the room; get my slides loaded on the computer; iron my shirt. I crossed off the things that were not important right then.

When faced with so many tasks and obligations that you can't figure out which to tackle first, stop. Take a deep breath. Get present in the moment and ask yourself what is most important this very second – not what's most important tomorrow or even an hour from now. If you're not sure, make a list of everything vying for your attention and cross off anything that is not important *right now*.

GET THE FUTURE OUT OF YOUR HEAD

Getting the future out of your head enables you to more fully focus on "what is important now." In this case, my next step was to sit down and list those things that might have been essential – just not right now. So I opened to another page in my journal. This time, I asked myself, "What might you want to do someday as a result of today?" This was not a list of firm commitments, just a way to get all of the ideas out of my head and on paper. This had two purposes. First, it ensured I wouldn't forget about those ideas, which might prove useful later. Second, it alleviated that stressful and distracting feeling that I needed to act upon them right this second.

PRIORITISE

After this I prioritised each list. Then I worked on each item on the "what is essential now" list one at a time. I just calmly worked through the list and erased each item when it was complete. By the time I went to sleep I had not only done all the things that needed to be executed at that moment, but I had executed them better and faster, because I was focused.

The Pause That Refreshes

Jeffrey A. Rodgers, an executive vice president at Cornish & Carey Commercial/Newmark Knight Frank, was once taught the simple idea of pausing to refresh. It began when Jeff realised that as he drove home from work each evening his mind was still focused on work-related projects. We all know this feeling. We may have left the office physically, but we are very much still there mentally, as our minds get caught in the endless loop of replaying the events of today and worrying about all the things we need to get done the following day.

So now, as he gets to the door of his house, he applies what he calls "the pause that refreshes." This technique is easy. He stops for just a moment. He closes his eyes. He breathes in and out once: deeply and slowly. As he exhales, he lets the work issues fall away. This allows him to walk through the front door to his family with more singleness of purpose. It supports the sentiment attributed to Lao Tzu: "In work, do what you enjoy. In family life, be completely present."

Thich Nhat Hanh, the Vietnamese Zen Buddhist monk who has been called the "world's calmest man," has spent a lifetime exploring how to live in *kairos,* albeit by a different name. He has taught it as mindfulness or maintaining "beginner's mind." He has written: "Mindfulness helps you go home to the present. And every time you go there and recognize a condition of happiness that you have, happiness comes."[2]

This focus on being in the moment affects the way he does everything. He takes a full hour to drink a cup of tea with the other monks every day. He explains: "Suppose you are drinking a cup of tea. When you hold your cup, you may like to breathe in, to bring your mind back to your body, and you become fully present. And when you are truly there, something else is also there – life, represented by the cup of tea. In that moment you are real, and the cup of tea is real. You are not lost in the past, in the future, in your projects, in your worries. You are free from all of these afflictions. And in that state of being free, you enjoy your tea. That is the moment of happiness, and of peace."

Pay attention through the day for your own *kairos* moments. Write them down in your journal. Think about what triggered that moment and what brought you out of it. Now that you know what triggers the moment, try to re-create it.

Training yourself to tune into *kairos* will not only enable you to achieve a higher level of contribution but also make you happier.

CHAPTER 20

BE

The Essentialist Life

BEWARE THE BARRENNESS OF A BUSY LIFE.

—*Socrates*

It all began while he was studying to become a barrister in England. With a wealthy family and good professional prospects, the future looked bright. Every day he woke up with a sense of certainty. He was clear on his main objective: to prepare to become a professional in law and then make a comfortable living. But then he took the opportunity to go on a journey around the world and everything changed.

Mohandas K. Gandhi went to South Africa and saw oppression there. Suddenly, he found a higher purpose: the liberation of the oppressed everywhere.

With this new singleness of purpose, he eliminated everything else from his life. He called the process "reducing himself to zero."[1] He dressed in his own homespun cloth *(khadi)* and inspired his followers to do the same. He spent three years not reading any newspapers because he found that their contents added only non-essential confusion to his life. He spent thirty-five years experimenting with simplifying his diet.[2] He spent a day each week without speaking. It would be an understatement to say he eschewed consumerism: when he died he owned fewer than ten items.

More importantly, of course, he devoted his life to helping the people of India gain independence. He intentionally never held a political position of any kind, yet he became, officially within India, the "Father of the Nation." But his contribution extended well beyond India. As General George C. Marshall, the American secretary of state, said on the occasion of Gandhi's passing: "Mahatma Gandhi had become the spokesman for the conscience of mankind, a man who made humility and simple truth more powerful than empires."[3] And Albert Einstein added: "Generations to come will scarce believe that such a one as this ever in flesh and blood walked upon this earth."[4]

It is impossible to argue with the statement that Gandhi lived a life that really mattered.

Of course, we don't have to try to replicate Gandhi to benefit from his example as someone who lived, fully and completely, as an Essentialist. We can all purge our lives of the non-essential and embrace the way of the Essentialist – in our own ways, and in our own time, and on our own scale. We can all live a life not just of simplicity but of high contribution and meaning.

Living Essentially

There are two ways of thinking about Essentialism. The first is to think of it as something you *do* occasionally. The second is to think of it as something you *are*. In the former, Essentialism is one more thing to add to your already overstuffed life. In the latter, it is a different way – a simpler way – of doing everything. It becomes a lifestyle. It becomes an all-encompassing approach to living and leading. It becomes the essence of who we are.

Essentialism has deep roots in many spiritual and religious traditions. Gautama Buddha left his life as a prince to seek the ascetic life. This led him to his enlightenment and the birth of Buddhism. Likewise, Judaism grew out of the story of Moses leaving his opulent life as an adopted prince in Egypt to live in the wilderness as a shepherd. It was there he encountered the burning bush and discovered his essential mission to bring the Israelites out of bondage. The Prophet Muhammad lived an essential life that included mending his own shoes and clothes and milking his own goat and taught his followers in Islam to do the same. John the Baptist, too, had the epitome of a simple lifestyle – living in the desert, wearing camel hair clothes, and eating off the land. Christian groups such as Quakers also maintained a staunchly Essentialist element to their faith: for example, they practised "the Testimony of Simplicity," in which they committed to a life of only what was essential. And of course Jesus lived as carpenter and then in his ministry lived without wealth, political position, or material belongings.

We can see the philosophy of "less but better" reflected in the lives of other notable and diverse figures – both religious and secular – throughout history: to name a few, the Dalai Lama, Steve Jobs, Leo Tolstoy, Michael Jordan, Warren Buffett, Mother Teresa, and Henry David Thoreau (who wrote, "I do believe in simplicity. It is astonishing as well as sad, how many trivial affairs even the wisest thinks he must attend to in a day; . . . so simplify the problem of life, distinguish the necessary and the real").[5]

Indeed, we can find Essentialists among the most successful people in every type of human endeavour. These include religious leaders, journalists, politicians, lawyers, doctors, investors, athletes, authors, artists. These people make their greatest contribution in many different ways. But they share one trait: they don't just give lip service to the idea of "less but better." They have *deliberately chosen to fully embrace the way of the Essentialist.*

Regardless of what job, field, or industry we are in, we can all choose to do the same.

Hopefully, at this point in the book, you've learned and absorbed all the core tenets and skills of an Essentialist. In this chapter, it's time to take that final step and learn how to use those skills not just to practice Essentialism occasionally but to *become* a true Essentialist.

MAJORING IN MINOR ACTIVITIES

There is a big difference between being a non-Essentialist who happens to apply Essentialist practices and an Essentialist who only occasionally slips back into some non-Essentialist practices. The question is, "Which is your major and which is your minor?" Most of us have a little Essentialist and a little non-Essentialist in us, but the question is, Which are you at the core?

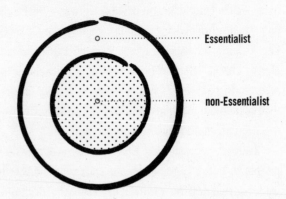

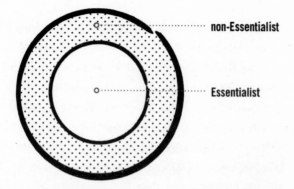

People with Essentialism at their core get far more from their investment than those who absorb it only at the surface level. Indeed, the benefits become cumulative. Every choice we make to pursue the essential and eliminate the non-essential builds on itself, making that choice more and more habitual until it becomes virtually second nature. With time, that inner core expands outwards until it has all but eclipsed the part of us still mired in the non-essential.

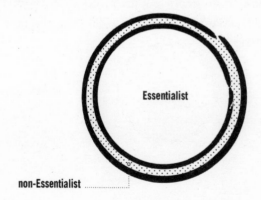

It is easy to get caught up in the "paradox of success" we discussed in chapter 1. We have clarity of purpose, which leads us to success. But with our success we get new options and opportunities. This sounds like a good thing, but remember, these options unintentionally distract us, tempt us, lure us away. Our clarity becomes clouded, and soon we find ourselves spread too thin. Now, instead of being utilised at our highest level of contribution, we make only a millimetre of progress in a million directions. Ultimately, our success becomes a catalyst for our failure. The only way out of this cycle is the way of the Essentialist.

But the way of the Essentialist isn't just about success; it's about living a life of meaning and purpose. When we look back on our careers and our lives, would we rather see a long laundry list of "accomplishments" that don't really matter or just a few major accomplishments that have real meaning and significance?

If you allow yourself to fully embrace Essentialism – to really live it, in everything you do, whether at home or at work – it can become a part of the way you see and understand the world. You can change your thinking so deeply that the practices of Essentialism we have discussed, and many others you will develop, become natural and instinctive:

As these ideas become emotionally true, they take on the power to change you.

The Greeks had a word, *metanoia,* that refers to a transformation of the heart. We tend to think of transformations as happening only in the mind. But as the proverb goes, "As a man thinketh *in his heart,* so is he" (italics added).[6] Once the essence of Essentialism enters our hearts, the way of the Essentialist becomes who we are. We become a different, better version of ourselves.

Once you become an Essentialist, you will find that you aren't like everybody else. When other people are saying yes, you will find yourself saying no. When other people are doing, you will find yourself thinking. When other people are speaking, you will find yourself listening. When other people are in the spotlight, vying for attention, you will find yourself waiting on the sidelines until it is time to shine. While other people are padding their résumés and building out their LinkedIn profiles, you will be building a career of meaning. While other people are complaining (read: bragging) about how busy they are, you will just be smiling sympathetically, unable to relate. While other people are living a life of stress and chaos, you will be living a life of impact and fulfilment. In many ways, to live as an Essentialist in our too-many-things-all-the-time society is an act of quiet revolution.

Living fully as an Essentialist isn't always easy. In many ways, I still struggle with it myself. I still instinctively want to please people when they ask me to do something, even something I know is non-Essential. When presented with opportunities – especially good opportunities – I still fall into thinking, "I can do both" when I really can't. I still fight the urge to impulsively check my phone; on my worst days I have wondered if my tombstone will read, "He checked e-mail." I'll be the first to admit, the transition doesn't happen overnight.

Still, over time I have found it gets easier and easier. Saying no feels less uncomfortable. Decisions get much clearer. Eliminating the non-Essentials becomes more natural and instinctive. I feel greater control of my choices, to the point that my life is different. If you open your heart and mind to embrace Essentialism fully, these things will become true for you as well.

Today Essentialism is not just something I do. An Essentialist is something I am steadily becoming. At first it was a few deliberate choices, then it grew into a lifestyle, and then it changed me, at my very core. I continue to discover almost daily that I can do less and less – in order to contribute more.

What being an Essentialist means to me is best illustrated in the little moments. It means:

- Choosing to wrestle with my children on the trampoline instead of going to a networking event
- Choosing to say no to international client work for the last year in order to write
- Choosing to set aside a day each week where I don't check any social media so I can be fully present at home
- Choosing to spend eight months getting up at 5 a.m. every morning and writing till 1 p.m. in order to finish this book
- Choosing to push back a work deadline in order to go camping with my children
- Choosing not to watch any television or movies when I travel for business so there is time to think and rest
- Choosing regularly to spend a whole day on that day's priority, even if it means doing nothing else on my to-do list
- Choosing to put the novel I am reading on hold because it is not the priority today
- Choosing to keep a journal almost every day for the last ten years
- Choosing to say no to a speaking opportunity in order to have a date night with Anna
- Choosing to exchange time on Facebook for a regular call with my ninety-three-year-old grandfather
- Choosing to turn down a recent offer to be a lecturer at Stanford University since I knew it meant time away from spreading the message of Essentialism through my lectures, and being with family

The list goes on, but the point I want to make here is that focusing on the essentials is a *choice*. It is *your* choice. That in itself is incredibly liberating.

Years ago, after I had quit law school, I was deciding what to do next in my career. With Anna as my sounding board, I explored dozens, perhaps hundreds, of different ideas. Then one day we were driving home and I said, "What if I went to Stanford for my graduate work?" There had been a lot of "What if?" questions like that. Usually the ideas just didn't stick. But this time I felt a sense of immediate clarity: in that instant, I just *knew*, even as the words escaped my lips, that this was the essential path for me.

What made me so sure I was on the right path was how the clarity disappeared when I even thought of applying elsewhere. Several times I started the application process for other courses but always stopped after a few minutes. It just didn't feel right. So I concentrated my efforts only on that single application. As I waited to hear back from the university, many other opportunities, some quite tempting, presented themselves. I said no to all of them. But despite the uncertainty of not yet knowing whether I had been accepted, I didn't feel anxious or nervous. Instead, I felt calm, focused, and in control.

I applied only to Stanford – both times. When I finally received my offer the second time round it couldn't have been more clear to me that this was the most vital thing for me to be doing. It was the right path at the right time. It was the quiet, personal confirmation of the way of the Essentialist.

Had I not chosen the path of the Essentialist, I might never have pursued the "Stanford or bust" strategy. I might never have written for *Harvard Business Review*. And I most certainly would never have written the words that you are now reading, absorbing, and hopefully thinking hard about how to integrate into your own life.

Becoming an Essentialist is a long process, but the benefits are endless. Here are some of the ways the disciplined pursuit of less can change your life for the better.

MORE CLARITY

Remember the metaphorical wardrobe we discussed in chapter 1? As you continue to clear out the wardrobe of your life, you will experience a reordering of what *really* matters. Life will become less about efficiently crossing off what was on your to-do list or rushing through everything on your schedule and more about changing what you put on there in the first place. Every day it becomes more clear than the day before how the essential things are so much more important than the next most important thing in line. As a result, the execution of those essentials becomes more and more effortless.

MORE CONTROL

You will gain confidence in your ability to pause, push back, or not rush in. You will feel less and less a function of other people's to-do lists and agendas. Remember that if you don't prioritise your life someone else will. But if you are determined to prioritise your own life you can. The power is yours. It is within you.

MORE JOY IN THE JOURNEY

With the focus on what is truly important *right now* comes the ability to live life more fully, in the moment. For me, a key benefit of being more present in the moment has been making joyful memories that would otherwise not exist. I smile more. I value simplicity. I am more joyful.

As the Dalai Lama, another true Essentialist, has said: "If one's life is simple, contentment has to come. Simplicity is extremely important for happiness."

The Essential Life: Living a Life That *Really* Matters

The life of an Essentialist is a life of meaning. It is a life that really matters.

When I need a reminder of this I think of a story. It is about a man whose three-year-old daughter died. In his grief he put together a video of her short little life. But as he went through all of his home videos he realised something was missing. He had taken video of every outing they had gone on and every trip they had taken. He had lots of footage – that wasn't the problem. But then he realised that while he had plenty of footage of the places they had gone – the sights they had seen, the views they had enjoyed, the meals they had eaten, and the landmarks they had visited – he had almost no close-up footage of his daughter herself. He had been so busy recording the surroundings he had failed to record what was essential.

This story captures the two most personal learnings that have come to me on the long journey of writing this book. The first is the exquisitely important role of my family in my life. At the very, very end, everything else will fade into insignificance by comparison. The second is the pathetically tiny amount of time we have left of our lives. For me this is not a depressing thought but a thrilling one. It removes fear of choosing the wrong thing. It infuses courage into my bones. It challenges me to be even more unreasonably selective about how to use this precious – and *precious* is perhaps too insipid a word – time. I know of someone who visits cemeteries around the world when he travels. I thought this was odd at first, but now I realise that this habit keeps his own mortality to the fore.

The life of an Essentialist is a life lived without regret. If you have correctly identified what really matters, if you invest your time and energy in it, then it is difficult to regret the choices you make. You become proud of the life you have chosen to live.

Will you choose to live a life of purpose and meaning, or will you look back on your one single life with twinges of regret? If you take one thing away from this book, I hope you will remember this: whatever decision or challenge or crossroads you face in your life, simply ask yourself, "What is essential?" Eliminate everything else.

If you are ready to look inside yourself for the answer to this question, then you are ready to commit to the way of the Essentialist.

Leadership Essentials

NEVER DOUBT THAT A SMALL GROUP OF THOUGHTFUL,
COMMITTED CITIZENS CAN CHANGE THE WORLD;
INDEED, IT'S THE ONLY THING THAT EVER HAS.

—*Margaret Mead*

LinkedIn CEO Jeff Weiner sees "fewer things done better" as *the* most powerful mechanism for leadership. When he took the reins of the company he could easily have adopted the standard operating procedure of most Silicon Valley start-ups and tried to pursue everything. Instead, he said no to really good opportunities in order to pursue only the very best ones. He uses the acronym FCS (a.k.a. FOCUS) to teach his philosophy to his employees. The letters stand for "Fewer things done better," "Communicating the right information to the right people at the right time," and "Speed and quality of decision making." Indeed, this is what it means to lead essentially.

ESSENTIALIST TEAMS

Essentialism as a way of thinking and acting is as relevant to the way we lead companies and teams as it is to the way we lead our lives. In fact, many of the ideas I have shared in this book first became clear to me in working with executive teams.

I have since gathered data from more than five hundred individuals about their experience on more than one thousand teams. I asked them to answer a series of questions about a time when they had worked on a *unified* team, what the experience was like, what role their manager played, and what the end result was. Then I got them to contrast this with a time when they had been on a *disunified* team and what that was like, what role their manager played, and how it affected the end result.

The results of this research were startling: when there was a high level of clarity of purpose, the team and the people in it overwhelmingly thrived. When there was a serious lack of clarity about what the team stood for and what their goals and roles were, people experienced confusion, stress, frustration, and ultimately failure. As one senior vice president succinctly summarised it when she looked at the results gathered from her extended team: "Clarity equals success."

This is just one of the many reasons that the principle of "less but better" is just as useful in building teams that can make a difference as it is in enabling individuals to live a life that really matters. Life in teams today is fast and full of opportunity. When teams are unified, the abundance of opportunity can be a good thing. But when teams lack clarity of purpose, it becomes difficult if not impossible to discern which of these myriad opportunities are truly vital. The unintended consequence is that non-Essentialist managers try to get their teams to pursue too many things – and try to do too many things themselves as well – and the team plateaus in its progress. An Essentialist leader makes a different choice. With clarity of purpose, she is able to apply "less but better" to everything from talent selection, to direction, to roles, to communication, to accountability. As a result her team becomes unified and breaks through to the next level.

THE ELEMENTS OF LEADING AS AN ESSENTIALIST

At this point in the book you've learned about flaws in non-Essentialist thinking and replaced that false logic with the basic truths of Essentialism. But Essentialism doesn't end with the individual. If you lead in any capacity – whether it's a team of two colleagues, a department of five hundred employees, or even some group in your school or community – the next step in your journey, if you are willing to take it, is to apply these same skills and mind-sets to your leadership.

	Non-Essentialist	**Essentialist**
MIND-SET	Everything to everyone	Less but better
TALENT	Hires people frantically and creates a "Bozo explosion."	Ridiculously selective on talent and removes people who hold the team back.
STRATEGY	Pursues a straddled strategy where everything is a priority.	Defines an essential intent by answering the question, "If we could only do one thing, what would it be?" Eliminates the non-essential distractions.
EMPOWERMENT	Allows ambiguity over who is doing what. Decisions are capricious.	Focuses on each team member's highest role and goal of contribution.
COMMUNICATION	Talks in code.	Listens to get to what is essential.
ACCOUNTABILITY	Checks in too much or is so busy he or she checks out altogether. Sometimes does both: disrupting the focus of the group and then being absent to the group.	Checks in with people in a gentle way to see how he or she can remove obstacles and enable small wins.
RESULT	A fractured team that makes a millimetre of progress in a million directions	A unified team that breaks through to the next level of contribution

From looking at this chart, the advantages of applying the Essentialist approach to every aspect of leadership that matters should be clear. Still, let's take a moment to briefly expand on these to get even clearer on how, exactly, to lead as an Essentialist.

BE RIDICULOUSLY SELECTIVE IN HIRING PEOPLE

A non-Essentialist tends to hire people frantically and impulsively – then gets too busy or distracted to either dismiss or reskill the people keeping the team back. At first the hiring bonanza seems justified because of the pace of growth that must be sustained. But in reality one wrong hire is far costlier than being one person short. And the cost of hiring *too many* wrong people (and one wrong hire often leads to multiple wrong hires because the wrong person will tend to attract more wrong people) is what Guy Kawasaki called a "Bozo explosion" – a term he uses to describe what happens when a formerly great team or company descends into mediocrity.[1]

An Essentialist, on the other hand, is ridiculously selective on talent. She has the discipline to hold out for the perfect hire – no matter how many CVs she has to read, or interviews she has to conduct, or talent searches she has to make – and doesn't hesitate to remove people who hold the team back. The result is a team full of all-star performers whose collective efforts add up to more than the sum of their parts (see chapter 9, "Select," for more on this subject).

DEBATE UNTIL YOU HAVE ESTABLISHED A REALLY CLEAR (NOT PRETTY CLEAR) ESSENTIAL INTENT

Without clarity of purpose, non-Essentialist leaders straddle their strategy: they try to pursue too many objectives and do too many things. As a result their teams get spread in a million directions and make little progress in any. They waste time on the non-essentials and neglect the things that really matter (see chapter

10 on the importance of purpose and essential intent). These days there is a lot of talk in organisations about "alignment," and indeed the more a team is aligned, the greater their contribution will be. Clear intent leads to alignment; vague direction produces misalignment every time.

GO FOR EXTREME EMPOWERMENT

The non-Essentialist disempowers people by allowing ambiguity over who is doing what. Often this is justified in the name of wanting to be a flexible or agile team. But what is actually created is a counterfeit agility. When people don't know what they are really responsible for and how they will be judged on their performance, when decisions either are or appear to be capricious, and when roles are ill-defined, it isn't long before people either give up or, worse, become obsessed with trying to look busy and therefore important instead of actually getting any real work done.

An Essentialist understands that clarity is the key to empowerment. He doesn't allow roles to be general and vague. He ensures that everyone in the team is *really* clear about what they are expected to contribute *and* what everyone else is contributing. One CEO recently admitted that he had allowed ambiguity in his executive team to keep the whole organisation back. To repair the damage, he said he went through a huge streamlining process until he was down to just four direct reports, each with a clear functional responsibility across the whole organisation.

The iconoclastic entrepreneur and venture capitalist Peter Thiel took "less but better" to an unorthodox level when he insisted that PayPal employees select one single priority in their role – and focus on that exclusively. As PayPal executive Keith Rabois recalls: "Peter required that everyone be tasked with exactly one priority. He would refuse to discuss virtually anything else with you except what was currently assigned as your No. 1 initiative. Even our annual review forms in 2001 required each employee to identify their single most valuable contribution to the company."[2] The result was the employees were empowered to do anything within the confines of that clearly defined role that they felt would make a high level of contribution to the shared mission of the company.

COMMUNICATE THE RIGHT THINGS TO THE RIGHT PEOPLE AT THE RIGHT TIME

The non-Essentialist leader communicates in code, and as a result people aren't sure what anything *really* means. Non-Essentialist communication usually is either too general to be actionable or changes so quickly that people are always caught off guard. Essentialist leaders, on the other hand, communicate the right things to the right people at the right time. Essentialist leaders speak succinctly, opting for restraint in their communication to keep the team focused. When they do speak, they are crystal clear. They eschew meaningless jargon, and their message is so consistent it seems almost boring to their ears. In this way, teams are able to pick up the essential through all the trivial noise.

CHECK IN OFTEN TO ENSURE MEANINGFUL PROGRESS

The non-Essentialist leader is not great on accountability. A primary and somewhat obvious reason is that the more items one pursues, the harder it is to follow up on all of them. In fact, a non-Essentialist leader may unintentionally train his people to expect no follow-up at all. In turn, the members of the team soon learn that there are no repercussions for failing, cutting corners, or prioritising what is easy over what is important. They learn that each objective pronounced by the leader will be emphasised only for a moment before giving way to something else of momentary interest.

By taking the time to get clear about the one thing that is really required, the Essentialist leader makes follow-up so easy and frictionless that it actually happens. By checking in with people frequently to reward small wins and help people remove obstacles, he bolsters the team's motivation and focus and enables them to make more meaningful progress (see chapter 17 on the power of progress).

Simply leading according to the principle of "less but better" will enable your team to amplify their level of collective contribution and achieve something truly remarkable.

As expressed by Ela Bhatt, a classic Essentialist and truly visionary leader whose legacy includes such meaningful achievements as winning the prestigious Indira Gandhi Prize for Peace, founding dozens of institutions dedicated to improving the conditions for poor women in India, and being named one of Hillary Clinton's personal heroines:

> Out of all virtues simplicity is my most favorite virtue. So much so that I tend to believe that simplicity can solve most of the problems, personal as well as the world problems. If the life approach is simple one need not lie so frequently, nor quarrel nor steal, nor envy, anger, abuse, kill. Everyone will have enough and plenty so need not hoard, speculate, gamble, hate. When character is beautiful, you are beautiful. That is the beauty of simplicity.[3]

Indeed that is the beauty of leading as an Essentialist.

Notes

1. THE ESSENTIALIST

1. A version of this story was published in a blog post I wrote for *Harvard Business Review* called "If You Don't Prioritize Your Life, Someone Else Will," June 28, 2012, http://blogs.hbr .org/2012/06/how-to-say-no-to-a-controlling/.

2. Originally called "the Clarity Paradox" in a blog post I wrote for *Harvard Business Review* called "The Disciplined Pursuit of Less," August 8, 2012, http://blogs.hbr.org/2012/08/the-disciplined-pursuit-of-less/. I have drawn from other *HBR* blogs I have written in various parts of this book.

3. Jim Collins, *How the Mighty Fall: And Why Some Companies Never Give In* (New York: HarperCollins, 2009).

4. Peter Drucker, "Managing Knowledge Means Managing Oneself," *Leader to Leader Journal,* no. 16 (Spring 2000), www.hesselbeininstitute.org/knowledgecenter/journal.aspx?ArticleID=26.

5. Shai Danziger, Jonathan Levav, and Liora Avnaim-Pessoa, "Extraneous Factors in Judicial Decisions," *Proceedings of the National Academy of Sciences* 108, no. 17 (2011): 6889–92.

6. Bronnie Ware, "The Top Five Regrets of the Dying," *Huffington Post,* January 21, 2012, www. huffingtonpost.com/bronnie-ware/top-5-regrets-of-the-dyin_b_1220965.html. I first wrote about this in a blog post I wrote for *Harvard Business Review* called "If You Don't Prioritize Your Life, Someone Else Will," June 28, 2012, http://blogs.hbr.org/2012/06/how-to-say-no-to-a-controlling/.

7. Ibid., "The Disciplined Pursuit of Less."

8. Ibid., "The Disciplined Pursuit of Less."

9. Peter Drucker interview with Bruce Rosenstein on April 11, 2005. Bruce wrote up the interview in his book *Living in More Than One World: How Peter Drucker's Wisdom Can Inspire and Transform Your Life* (San Francisco, CA: Berrett-Koehler, 2009).

10. *Race to Nowhere: The Dark Side of America's Achievement Culture* (dir. Vicki Abeles, 2011) is a documentary and a movement in schools working to fight, using my own words, non-Essentialism in school. They are working to reduce the imposition of unnecessary homework and stress on children. See their website, www.racetonowhere.com/.

11. There are many citations for this or similar statements. Emile Gauvreau is just one example: "I was part of that strange race of people aptly described as spending their lives doing things they detest, to make money they don't want, to buy things they don't need, to impress people they don't like" (quoted in Jay Friedenberg, *Artificial Psychology: The Quest for What It Means to Be Human* [New York: Taylor and Francis, 2010], 217).

12. Mary Oliver, "The Summer Day," in *New and Selected Poems,* vol. 1 (Boston: Beacon Press, 1992), 94.

2. CHOOSE

1. M. E. P. Seligman, "Learned Helplessness," *Annual Review of Medicine* 23, no. 1 (1972): 407–12, doi: 10.1146/annurev.me.23.020172.002203.

2. William James, *Letters of William James,* ed. Henry James (Boston: Atlantic Monthly Press, 1920), 1:147; quoted in Ralph Barton Perry, *The Thought and Character of William James* (1948; repr., Cambridge, MA: Harvard University Press, 1996), 1:323.

3. DISCERN

1. John Carlin, "If the World's Greatest Chef Cooked for a Living, He'd Starve," *Guardian,* December 11, 2006, http://observer.theguardian.com/foodmonthly/futureoffood/story/0,,1969713,00.
html.

2. Joseph Moses Juran, *Quality-Control Handbook* (New York: McGraw Hill, 1951).

3. I originally wrote this in a blog post for the *Harvard Business Review,* called "The Unimportance of Practically Everything," May 29, 2012.

4. Richard Koch, *The 80/20 Principle: The Secret of Achieving More with Less* (London: Nicholas Brealey, 1997); *The Power Laws* (London: Nicholas Brealey, 2000), published in the United States as *The Natural Laws of Business* (New York: Doubleday, 2001); *The 80/20 Revolution* (London: Nicholas Brealey, 2002), published in the United States as *The 80/20 Individual* (New York: Doubleday, 2003); and *Living the 80/20 Way* (London: Nicholas Brealey, 2004).

5. Warren Buffett, quoted in Koch, *The 80/20 Individual,* 20.

6. Mary Buffett and David Clark, *The Tao of Warren Buffett: Warren Buffett's Words of Wisdom* (New York: Scribner, 2006), no. 68.

7. Ibid., "The Unimportance of Practically Everything."

8. At a meeting we both attended at the Bill and Melinda Gates Foundation in Seattle, Washington. He was speaking, and afterwards we chatted for a few minutes. He confirmed that he had said it or words to the same effect and that he certainly believed it was true.

9. John Maxwell, *Developing the Leader Within You* (Nashville, TN: T. Nelson, 1993), 22–23.

4. TRADE-OFF

1. "30-Year Super Stocks: Money Magazine Finds the Best Stocks of the Past 30 Years," *Money* magazine, October 9, 2002.

2. "Herb Kelleher: Managing in Good Times and Bad," interview, *View from the Top,* April 15, 2006, www.youtube.com/watch?v=wxyC3Ywb9yc.

3. M. E. Porter, "What Is Strategy?" *Harvard Business Review* 74, no. 6 (1996).

4. Erin Callan, "Is There Life After Work?" *New York Times,* March 9, 2013.

5. Judith Rehak, "Tylenol Made a Hero of Johnson & Johnson," *New York Times,* March 23, 2002, www.nytimes.com/2002/03/23/your-money/23iht-mjj_ed3_.html.

6. Michael Josephson, "Business Ethics Insight: Johnson & Johnson's Values-Based Ethical Culture: Credo Goes Beyond Compliance," *Business Ethics and Leadership,* February 11, 2012, http://josephsoninstitute.org/business/blog/2012/02/business-ethics-insight-johnson-johnsons-values-based-ethical-culture-its-credo-goes-beyond-compliancer-than-compliance-based-rules-culture/.

7. Sowell in a talk he gave at Ohio State University in 1992.

8. Stephanie Smith, "Jim Collins on Creating Enduring Greatness," *Success,* n.d., www.success.com/articles/1003-jim-collins-on-creating-enduring-greatness, accessed September 22, 2013.

9. David Sedaris, "Laugh, Kookaburra," *The New Yorker,* August 24, 2009, www.newyorker.com/reporting/2009/08/24/090824fa_fact_sedaris.

5. ESCAPE

1. Frank O'Brien, "Do-Not-Call Mondays."

2. Scott Doorley and Scott Witthoft, *Make Space: How to Set the Stage for Creative Collaboration* (Hoboken, NJ: John Wiley, 2012), 132.

3. Richard S. Westfall, *Never at Rest: A Biography of Isaac Newton* (Cambridge: Cambridge University Press, 1980), 105.

4. Jeff Weiner, "The Importance of Scheduling Nothing," *LinkedIn,* April 3, 2013, https://www.linkedin.com/today/post/article/20130403215758-22330283-the-importance-of-scheduling-nothing.

5. I am indebted here to an excellent first-person account of Bill Gates's Think Week by Robert A. Guth, "In Secret Hideaway, Bill Gates Ponders Microsoft's Future," *Wall Street Journal,* March 28, 2005, http://online.wsj.com/article/0,,SB111196625830690477,00.html.

6. LOOK

1. Nora Ephron, "The Best Journalism Teacher I Ever Had," *Northwest Scholastic Press,* June 18, 2013, www.nwscholasticpress.org/2013/06/18/the-best-journalism-teacher-i-ever-had/#sthash.ZFtUBv50.dpbs; also written about by Ephron in her essay "Getting to the

Point," in *Those Who Can . . . Teach! Celebrating Teachers Who Make a Difference,* by Lorraine Glennon and Mary Mohler (Berkeley, CA: Wildcat Canyon Press, 1999), 95–96.

2. Accident description in the Aviation Safety Network's Aviation Safety Database, http://aviation-safety.net/database/, accessed June 9, 2012.

3. To Harry Potter in the film, *Deathly Hallows – Part 1.*

4. "The game is to have them all running about with fire extinguishers when there is a flood, and all crowding to that side of the boat which is already nearly gunwale under." C. S. Lewis, *The Screwtape Letters* (San Francisco, CA: HarperCollins, 2001), 138.

5. "Young Firm Saves Babies' Lives," Stanford Graduate School of Business, June 7, 2011, www.stanford.edu/group/knowledgebase/cgi-bin/2011/06/07/young-firm-saves-babies-lives/.

7. PLAY

1. Mihaly Csikszentmihalyi, *Flow, the Secret to Happiness,* TED talk, February 2004, video, www.ted.com/talks/mihaly_csikszentmihalyi_on_flow.html.

2. Sir Ken Robinson, *Bring on the Learning Revolution!,* TED talk, February 2010, video, www.ted.com/talks/sir_ken_robinson_bring_on_the_revolution.html.

3. Stuart Brown, *Play Is More Than Just Fun,* TED talk, May 2008, video, www.ted.com/talks/stuart_brown_says_play_is_more_than_fun_it_s_vital.html.

4. Quoted in Stuart Brown, *Play: How It Shapes the Brain, Opens the Imagination, and Invigorates the Soul* (New York: Avery, 2009), 29.

5. Jaak Panksepp, *Affective Neuroscience: The Foundations of Human and Animal Emotions* (Oxford: Oxford University Press, 1998), 297.

6. Quoted as conversation between Einstein and János Plesch in János Plesch's *János: The Story of a Doctor,* trans. Edward FitzGerald (London: Gollancz, 1947), 207.

7. Supriya Ghosh, T. Rao Laxmi, and Sumantra Chattarji, "Functional Connectivity from the Amygdala to the Hippocampus Grows Stronger after Stress," *Journal of Neuroscience* 33, no. 38 (2013), abstract, www.jneurosci.org/content/33/17/7234.abstract.

8. Edward M. Hallowell, *Shine: Using Brain Science to Get the Best from Your People* (Boston: Harvard Business Review Press, 2011), 125.

9. Ibid., p. 113.

8. SLEEP

1. K. Anders Ericsson, Ralf Th. Krampe, and Clemens Tesch-Romer, "The Role of Deliberate Practice in the Acquisition of Expert Performance," *Psychological Review* 100, no. 3 (1993): 363–406, http://graphics8.nytimes.com/images/blogs/freakonomics/pdf/DeliberatePractice(PsychologicalReview).pdf.

2. Charles A. Czeisler, "Sleep Deficit: The Performance Killer," interview by Bronwyn Fryer, *Harvard Business Review,* October 2006, http://hbr.org/2006/10/sleep-deficit-the-performance-killer.

3. Ullrich Wagner et al., "Sleep Inspires Insight," *Nature* 427 (January 22, 2004): 352–55. An additional study further supports the idea: Michael Hopkin, "Sleep Boosts Lateral Thinking," *Nature* online, January 22, 2004, www.nature.com/news/2004/040122/full/news040119-10.html.

4. Nancy Ann Jeffrey, "Sleep Is the New Status Symbol For Successful Entrepreneurs," *Wall Street Journal,* April 2, 1999, http://online.wsj.com/article/SB923008887262090895.html.

5. Erin Callan, "Is There Life After Work?," *New York Times,* March 9, 2013, www.nytimes.com/2013/03/10/opinion/sunday/is-there-life-after-work.html?_r=0.

9. SELECT

1. Derek Sivers, "No More Yes. It's Either HELL YEAH! or No," August 26, 2009, http://sivers.org/hellyeah.

2. "Box CEO Levie at Startup Day," *GeekWire,* September 24, 2012, https://www.youtube.com/watch?v=W99AjxpUff8.

3. I originally cited this in a blog post I wrote for *Harvard Business Review* called "The Disciplined Pursuit of Less," August 8, 2012, http://blogs.hbr.org/2012/08/the-disciplined-pursuit-of-less/.

10. CLARIFY

1. This exercise and other parts of this chapter were originally published in *Harvard Business Review* called "If I Read One More Platitude-Filled Mission Statement, I'll Scream," October 4, 2012.

2. I am indebted here to Gary Hamel and C. K. Prahalad and their brilliant piece in *Harvard Business Review,* "Strategic Intent," May 1989, http://hbr.org/1989/05/strategic-intent/ar/1. They use as context the Japanese companies at the time who had a long-term intent to stretch companies to go beyond their current level of resources. Over time as I have worked with people and teams this idea has proven useful but has changed sufficiently enough to be described differently. Thus an essential intent.

11. DARE

1. Juan Williams, *Eyes on the Prize: America's Civil Rights Years, 1954–1965* (New York: Penguin Books, 2002), 66.

2. Mark Feeney, "Rosa Parks, Civil Rights Icon, Dead at 92," *Boston Globe,* October 25, 2005.

3. Donnie Williams and Wayne Greenhaw, *The Thunder of Angels: The Montgomery Bus Boycott and the People who Broke the Back of Jim Crow* (Chicago: Chicago Review Press, 2005), 48.

4. "Civil Rights Icon Rosa Parks Dies at 92," CNN, October 25, 2005.

5. This story is shared in a few different places, but this account is taken from my interview with Cynthia Covey in 2012.

6. Stephen R. Covey and Roger and Rebecca Merrill, *First Things First* (New York: Simon and Schuster, 1995), 75.

7. http://wps.prenhall.com/hssaronsonsocpsych6/64/16428/4205685.cw/-/4205769/index.html.

8. Quoted in Howard Gardner, "Creators: Multiple Intelligences," in *The Origins of Creativity*, ed. Karl H. Pfenninger and Valerie R. Shubik (Oxford: Oxford University Press, 2001), 132.

9. First referenced in a blog post I wrote for *Harvard Business Review* called "If You Don't Prioritize Your Life, Someone Else Will," June 28, 2012, http://blogs.hbr.org/2012/06/how-to-say-no-to-a-controlling/

10. In *1993 Interview re: Paul Rand and Steve Jobs*, dir. Doug Evans, uploaded January 7, 2007, www.youtube.com/watch?v=xb8idEf-lak, Steve Jobs shares how Paul Rand came up with the logo for NeXT.

11. Carol Hymowitz, "Kay Krill on Giving Ann Taylor a Makeover," *Business Week*, August 9, 2012, www.businessweek.com/articles/2012-08-09/kay-krill-on-giving-ann-taylor-a-makeover#p2.

12. UNCOMMIT

1. "Concorde the Record Breaker," n.d., www.concorde-art-world.com/html/record_breaker.html, accessed September 22, 2013; Peter Gillman, "Supersonic Bust," *Atlantic*, January 1977, www.theatlantic.com/past/docs/issues/77jan/gillman.htm.

2. "Ministers Knew Aircraft Would Not Make Money," *Independent*, http://www.independent.co.uk/news/uk/ministers-knew-aircraft-would-not-make-money-concorde-thirty-years-ago-harold-macmillan-sacked-a-third-of-his-cabinet-concorde-was-approved-the-cuba-crisis-shook-the-world-and-ministers-considered-pit-closures-anthony-bevins-and-nicholas-timmins-review-highlights-from-1962-government-files-made-public-yesterday-1476025.html

3. Peter Gillman, "Supersonic Bust." theatlantic.com/issues/77jan/gillman.htm

4. Michael Rosenfield, "NH Man Loses Life Savings on Carnival Game," CBS Boston, April 29, 2013, http://boston.cbslocal.com/2013/04/29/nh-man-loses-life-savings-on-carnival-game/.

5. Daniel Kahneman, Jack L. Knetsch, and Richard H. Thaler, "Anomalies: The Endowment Effect, Loss Aversion, and Status Quo Bias," *Journal of Economic Perspective* 5, no. 1 (1991): 193–206, http://users.tricity.wsu.edu/~achaudh/kahnemanetal.pdf.

6. Tom Stafford, "Why We Love to Hoard . . . and How You Can Overcome It," BBC News, July 17, 2012, www.bbc.com/future/story/20120717-why-we-love-to-hoard.

7. I originally wrote this in a blog post for *Harvard Business Review* called "The Disciplined Pursuit of Less," August 8, 2012, http://blogs.hbr.org/2012/08/the-disciplined-pursuit-of-less/.

8. Hal R. Arkes and Peter Aykon, "The Sunk Cost and Concorde Effects: Are Humans Less Rational Than Lower Animals?" *Psychological Bulletin* 125, no. 5 (1999): 591–600, http://americandreamcoalition-org.adcblog.org/transit/sunkcosteffect.pdf.

9. James Surowiecki, "That Sunk-Cost Feeling," *The New Yorker,* January 21, 2013, www. newyorker. com/talk/financial/2013/01/21/130121ta_talk_surowiecki.

10. Daniel Shapero, "Great Managers Prune as Well as Plant," LinkedIn, December 13, 2012, www. linkedin.com/today/post/article/20121213073143-314058-great-managers-prune-as-well-as -plant.

13. EDIT

1. Mark Harris, "Which Editing Is a Cut Above?" *New York Times,* January 6, 2008. In 1980, *Ordinary People* won as Best Picture, but its editor Jeff Kanew was not nominated for Best Editing.

2. March Harris, "Which Editing."

3. "Jack Dorsey: The CEO as Chief Editor," February 9, 2011, video, uploaded February 15, 2011, www.youtube.com/watch?v=fs0R-UvZ-hQ.

4. Stephen King, *On Writing: A Memoir of the Craft,* 10th Anniversary ed. (New York: Pocket Books, 2000), 224.

5. I wrote about this subject further in a blog post for *Harvard Business Review* called "The One Thing CEOs Need to Learn from Apple," April 30, 2012.

6. King, third foreword to Ibid., xix.

7. Alan D. Williams, "What Is an Editor?" in *Editors on Editing: What Writers Need to Know About What Editors Do,* 3rd rev. ed., ed. Gerald Gross (New York: Grove Press, 1993), 6.

14. LIMIT

1. Some minor details changed.

2. Based on a talk Clayton Christensen gave to students at the Stanford Law School in 2013.

3. Henry Cloud and John Townsend, *Boundaries: When to Say Yes, How to Say No* (Grand Rapids, MI: Zondervan, 1992), 29–30.

4. I have found this story cited in several places: for example, Jill Rigby's *Raising Respectful Children in an Unrespectful World* (New York: Simon & Schuster, 2006), ch. 6. But I have yet to find an original source for the story and therefore share this only as an anecdote.

15. BUFFER

1. Guy Lodge, "Thatcher and North Sea Oil: A Failure to Invest in Britain's Future," *New Statesman,* April 15, 2013, www.newstatesman.com/politics/2013/04/thatcher-and-north-sea-oil-%E2%80%93-failure-invest-britain%E2%80%99s-future.

2. Dale Hurd, "Save or Spend? Norway's Commonsense Example," CBN News, July 11, 2011, www.cbn.com/cbnnews/world/2011/July/Save-or-Spend-Norways-Common-Sense-Example-/.

3. Richard Milne, "Debate Heralds Change for Norway's Oil Fund," FT.com, June 30, 2013, www.ft.com/cms/s/0/8466bd90-e007-11e2-9de6-00144feab7de.html#axzz2ZtQp4H13.

4. See Roland Huntford, *The Last Place on Earth: Scott and Amundsen's Race to the South Pole* (New York: Modern Library, 1999).

5. Jim Collins and Morten T. Hansen, *Great by Choice: Uncertainty, Chaos, and Luck – Why Some Thrive Despite Them All* (New York: Harper Business, 2011).

6. Daniel Kahneman and Amos Tversky, "Intuitive Prediction: Biases and Corrective Procedures," *TIMS Studies in Management Science* 12 (1979): 313–27.

7. Roger Buehler, Dale Griffin, and Michael Ross, "Exploring the 'Planning Fallacy: Why People Underestimate Their Task Completion Times," *Journal of Personality and Social Psychology* 67, no. 3 (1994): 366–81, doi:10.1037/0022-3514.67.3.366.

8. Roger Buehler, Dale Griffin, and Michael Ross, "Inside the Planning Fallacy: The Causes and Consequences of Optimistic Time Predictions," in *Heuristics and Biases: The Psychology of Intuitive Judgment,* ed. Thomas Gilovich, Dale Griffin, and Daniel Kahneman (Cambridge: Cambridge University Press, 2002), 250–70.

9. Stephanie P. Pezzo, Mark V. Pezzo, and Eric R. Stone, "The Social Implications of Planning: How Public Predictions Bias Future Plans," *Journal of Experimental Social Psychology* 42 (2006): 221–27.

10. Global Facility for Disaster Reduction and Recovery, "Protecting Morocco through Integrated and Comprehensive Risk Management," n.d., www.gfdrr.org/sites/gfdrr.org/files/Pillar_1_ Protecting_Morocco_through_Integrated_and_Comprehensive_Risk_Management.pdf, accessed September 22, 2013.

11. Also in this piece he identifies twelve reasons people don't practise risk mitigation: Wharton Center for Risk Management and Decision Processes, "Informed Decisions on Catastrophe Risk," Wharton Issue Brief, Winter 2010, http://opim.wharton.upenn.edu/risk/library/ WRCib20101_PsychNatHaz.pdf.

16. SUBTRACT

1. Eliyahu M. Goldratt, *The Goal: A Process of Ongoing Improvement* (Great Barrington, MA: North River Press, 2004), ch. 13, p. 94.

2. Sigmund Krancberg, *A Soviet Postmortem: Philosophical Roots of the "Grand Failure"* (Lanham, MD: Rowman and Littlefield, 1994), 56.

3. en.wikipedia.org/wiki/poiesi.

17. PROGRESS

1. Parts of this chapter were first published in a blog post I wrote for *Harvard Business Review* called "Can We Reverse The Stanford Prison Experiment?" June 12, 2012.

2. Based on my interviews with Ward Clapham between 2011 and 2013.

3. Speech at the annual Labour Party Conference, September 30, 1993, when Blair was shadow home secretary; see "Not a Time for Soundbites: Tony Blair in Quotations," *Oxford University Press Blog,* June 29, 2007, http://blog.oup.com/2007/06/tony_blair/#sthash.P1rl6OHy.dpuf.

4. Frederick Herzberg, "One More Time: How Do You Motivate Employees?" *Harvard Business Review,* September–October 1987, www.facilitif.eu/user_files/file/herzburg_article.pdf.

5. Teresa M. Amabile and Steven J. Kramer, "The Power of Small Wins," *Harvard Business Review*, May 2011, http://hbr.org/2011/05/the-power-of-small-wins/.

6. "The Lord Will Multiply the Harvest," An Evening with Henry B. Eyring, February 6, 1998. http://www.lds.org/manual/teaching-seminary-preservice-readings-religion-370-471-and-475/the-lord-will-multiply-the-harvest?lang=eng.

7. Ibid., "Can we reverse the Stanford Prison Experiment?".

8. See his website, http://heroicimagination.org/.

9. We got this idea from Glenn I. Latham's *The Power of Positive Parenting* (North Logan, UT: P&T Ink, 1994).

10. Seen on the wall on Facebook.

11. Popularised by Eric Ries in an interview at Venture Hacks, March 23, 2009, "What Is the Minimum Viable Product?" http://venturehacks.com/articles/minimum-viable-product.

12. Peter Sims, "Pixar's Motto: Going from Suck to Nonsuck," *Fast Company*, March 25, 2011, www
.fastcompany.com/1742431/pixars-motto-going-suck-nonsuck.

18. FLOW

1. Michael Phelps and Alan Abrahamson, *No Limits: The Will to Succeed* (New York: Free Press, 2008).

2. Charles Duhigg, *The Power of Habit: Why We Do What We Do in Life and Business* (New York: Random House, 2012).

3. Phelps and Abrahamson, *No Limits*.

4. "Plasticity in Neural Networks," in "The Brain from Top to Bottom," n.d., http://thebrain.mcgill.ca/flash/d/d_07/d_07_cl/d_07_cl_tra/d_07_cl_tra.html, accessed September 22, 2013.

5. "Habits: How They Form and How to Break Them," NPR, March 5, 2012, www.npr.org/2012/03/05/147192599/habits-how-they-form-and-how-to-break-them.

6. Mihaly Csikszentmihalyi, *Creativity: Flow and the Psychology of Discovery and Invention* (New York: Harper Perennial, 1997), 145.

7. David T. Neal, Wendy Wood, and Jeffrey M. Quinn, "Habit: A Repeat Performance," *Current Directions in Psychological Science* 15, no. 4 (2006): 198–202, http://web.archive.org/web/20120417115147/http://dornsife.usc.edu/wendywood/research/documents/Neal.Wood.Quinn.2006.pdf.

8. In an interview with Dan Pink, http://www.danpink.com/2012/03/the-power-of-habits-and-the-power-to-change-them/.

9. Stacy Cowley, "A Guide to Jack Dorsey's 80-Hour Workweek," CNNMoneyTech, November 14, 2011, http://money.cnn.com/2011/11/13/technology/dorsey_techonomy/index.htm.

19. FOCUS

1. *Jiro Dreams of Sushi*, dir. David Geld (2011).

2. "Oprah Talks to Thich Nhat Hanh," *O* magazine, March 2010, www.oprah.com/spirit/Oprah-Talks-to-Thich-Nhat-Hanh/3.

20. BE

1. Eknath Easwaran, preface to *The Essential Gandhi: An Anthology of His Writings on His Life, Work, and Ideas,* ed. Louis Fischer (1962; repr., New York: Vintage, 1990), xx.

2. "Gandhiji's Philosophy: Diet and Diet Programme," n.d., Mahatma Gandhi Information Website, www.gandhi-manibhavan.org/gandhiphilosophy/philosophy_health_dietprogramme.htm.

3. library.thinkquest.org/26523/mainfiles/quotes.htm.

4. Albert Einstein, "Mahatma Gandhi," in *Out of My Later Years: Essays* (New York: Philosophical Library, 1950).

5. Henry David Thoreau to H. G. O. Blake, March 27, 1848, in *The Portable Thoreau,* ed. Jeffrey S. Cramer (London: Penguin, 2012).

6. Proverbs 23:7.

APPENDIX: LEADERSHIP ESSENTIALS

1. Guy Kawasaki, "From the Desk of Management Changes at Apple," *MacUser,* December 1991, and then a follow-up piece, "How to Prevent a Bozo Explosion," *How to Change the World,* February 26, 2006, http://blog.guykawasaki.com/2006/02/how_to_prevent_.html.

2. Keith Rabois, answer to "What Strong Beliefs on Culture for Entrepreneurialism Did Peter/Max/David Have at PayPal?" Quora, n.d., www.quora.com/PayPal/What-strong-beliefs-on-culture-for-entrepreneurialism-did-Peter-Max-David-have-at-PayPal/answer/Keith-Rabois, accessed September 22, 2013.

3. From an e-mail and follow-up phone interview in August 2013.

Acknowledgements

Thank you to the following people:

Anna: for believing in this project for many years. And believing in me even longer. With this, as with everything, you have been my closest friend and my wisest counsellor.

Talia Krohn: for masterfully editing out the non-essential until only the essential remained.

Tina Constable, Tara Gilbride, Ayelet Gruenspecht, and Gianni Sandri: for starting a conversation *and* a movement.

Wade Lucas and Robin Wolfson: for taking Essentialism "on tour."

Rafe Sagalyn: for absolutely delivering on your A++ reputation as an agent.

Mum and Dad: for, you know, *everything*.

Nanny and Grandad: for showing us all what an essential life looks like.

Mom and Dad: for Anna.

Mrs Sweet: for teaching *me*.

Mr Frost: for making us *really* think.

Sam, James, Joseph, Lewis, and Craig: for liberating me to be myself. Consider this my "note to explain everything."

Amy Hayes: for making the whole journey one long win/win.

Justin: for reading various parts of this, in various forms, at various times of night and day.

Daniel, Deborah, Ellie, Louise, Max, Spencer, and Ruth: for making my choices easier by first seeing yours.

Britton, Jessica, John, Joseph, Lindsey, Megan, Whitney: for your unfailing support.

Rob and Natalie Maynes: for the gift of unfiltered conversation.

Peter Conti-Brown: for our "deal."

Allison Bebo, Jennifer Bailey, Tim Brown, Bob Carroll (Jr. and Sr.), Doug Crandall, Alyssa Friedrich, Tom Friel, Rocky Garff, Larry Gelwix, Jonathan Hoyt, Lila Ibrahim, PK, Jade Koyle, Lindsey LaTesta, Jared Lucas, Jim Meeks, Brian Miller, Greg Pal, Joel Podolny, Bill Rielly, Ash Solar, Andrew Sypkes, Shawn Vanderhoven, Jeff Weiner, Jake White, Eric Wong, Dave Yick, Ray Zinn, the entire YGL family, and the GSB class of 08: for bringing joy to the journey.

Stephen Covey and Steve Jobs: for inspiring me.

God: for planting in me this endless wish – and for granting it.

Index

Taking Essentialism Beyond the Page

As part of his engaging keynote speeches, talks, and workshops, Greg McKeown shares a strategic framework for living and leading as an Essentialist. Using real-world examples, Greg McKeown challenges assumptions and moves his audiences to action. Among his lecture topics are:

THE DISCIPLINED PURSUIT OF LESS (BUT BETTER) – *KEYNOTE*

This lecture speaks to anyone who has ever felt overworked but underutilised, or always busy but never productive. Greg McKeown offers a framework for discerning what is essential, eliminating what is not, and removing obstacles in order to make the execution of what is essential as effortless as possible. The disciplined pursuit of less allows employees to channel their time, energy, and effort towards making the highest possible contribution to what really matters.

LEADING AS AN ESSENTIALIST – *KEYNOTE*

In this keynote, Greg McKeown illustrates why leading as an Essentialist can help organisations accomplish more with fewer resources, take teams to the next level, and produce breakthroughs in results and innovation.

APPLYING ESSENTIALISM – THE LEADERSHIP DEVELOPMENT TRAINING

In this workshop, McKeown gives participants the tools to define the Strategic Intent of their business. Specifically, they will learn to Evaluate the trivial many from the vital few, Eliminate the non-essentials, and to Enable the team to almost effortlessly execute on the essentials.